The Adv of Sherl Holmes

CW00690419

Study Guide by Course Hero

What's Inside

👁 Book Basics

AUTHOR
Arthur Conan Doyle

YEAR PUBLISHED
1892

GENRE
Adventure

PERSPECTIVE AND NARRATOR
The events in *The Adventures of Sherlock Holmes* are narrated in the first person by the character Dr. John Watson, who conveys information about himself only insofar as it relates to the main figure of his narrative: Sherlock Holmes. Dr. Watson's admiration for Sherlock Holmes makes Watson a biased narrator.

TENSE
The Adventures of Sherlock Holmes is written in the past tense.

ABOUT THE TITLE
The Adventures of Sherlock Holmes, a collection of 12 short stories featuring the famous fictional detective Sherlock Holmes, was not the reading public's first introduction to the character. The stories in this collection were preceded by *A Study in Scarlet* (1888), *The Sign of Four* (1890), and a serialized set of magazine stories. By the time *The Adventures of Sherlock Holmes* was published, the character was wildly popular with the public. Hence, Doyle decided to include the character's name in the title as a way to boost sales.

⊘ In Context

The Victorian Era

Like his most famous literary creation Sherlock Holmes, Arthur Conan Doyle was a product of the Victorian era. Named for Queen Victoria, the British monarch who reigned from 1837 to 1901, the age coincided with a consolidation of British power and unprecedented advances in science, medicine, and the arts.

There were dramatic social changes as well. The growth of industry and train travel accelerated economic development, and cities—particularly London—became the center of British economic and cultural life. This new, globalized, increasingly urban order brought with it no small number of problems, and thinkers such as Herbert Spencer, John Stuart Mill, and Karl Marx, among others, devoted their time to writing books and essays advocating solutions, albeit drastically different ones.

Doyle was successful in developing many characters from different walks of Victorian British life. Some are more one-dimensional than others—in particular, people from the lower class and people of foreign origin—but many are remarkably lifelike.

The Rise of Empiricism

In 1859, the year Doyle was born, Charles Darwin published his landmark work on evolution, *On the Origin of Species*. The book laid the foundation for evolutionary biology and helped usher in a new era of scientific belief. It rejected supernatural or divine explanations, relying instead on observable evidence. This trend had a profound effect on public philosophy and medicine. For one, evolution challenged religious literalism, and it caused a crisis of faith among many Victorian writers, thinkers, and ordinary people. Darwin's deductive methodology paved the way for the advances in science, medicine, and public health in the coming years as well.

Holmes is the embodiment of the new Darwinian man. He has an obsessive reliance on "data" and has an exceptionally well-honed talent for observation. He is neither religious nor superstitious, and his default mode is skepticism—especially when confronted with suspects who seem obviously guilty in the eyes of Dr. John Watson and others.

The Rise of the City

London had been the largest city in the world since 1815, but between 1861 and 1920 its population exploded from three million people to more than seven million. By the early 20th century the city "formed an urban machine for living that was unprecedented in human history." This "urban machine" is the setting for most of the stories in *The Adventures of Sherlock Holmes*. In its pages the reader meets beggars, bankers, opium-den frequenters, lawyers, common thieves, gas fitters, engineers, ne'er-do-wells, administrative assistants, and many other modern creatures still present today.

While the city brought many ills—works such as Charles Dickens's *A Tale of Two Cities*, for example, illustrate them clearly—Victorian Britain also created a substantial middle class. In fact scholars have argued the Sherlock Holmes series reflects middle-class anxieties about social status and crime in the city. In a review of the book *Holmes & Social Order*, one critic writes that shifts in attitudes toward crime and other aspects of urban living "were due in the most part to the rise of the middle class and its desire to maintain public order, exalt the worth of work over inheritance, and claim social prestige for its accomplishments." With his sophisticated mind, solid upbringing, and Baker Street home, Sherlock Holmes is undoubtedly a member of the middle class, if not the urban elite.

This new middle class sharply increased the demand for newspapers and magazines. This is evident in Sherlock Holmes stories, as Holmes is constantly reading "the papers," and the detective keeps clippings of old crime sections in his archives. In real life this huge new market helped propel Doyle's success, as *The Strand Magazine* was the vehicle delivering the Holmes stories to a large audience.

ⓥ Author Biography

Arthur Conan Doyle was born to a Catholic family in Edinburgh, Scotland, on May 22, 1859. His father, Charles Altamont Doyle, was an artist and the son of John Doyle, a famous political cartoonist and London society fixture. At age 23 Charles married Mary Josephine Foley, who was just 17 when they wed. Seven of Charles and Mary's nine children survived through infancy.

Arthur had a chaotic childhood; Charles didn't make enough money to adequately support the family, and he became an alcoholic. Arthur received a good education with the help of financial assistance from his relatives, but he hated the strict and often violent disciplinary measures enforced at the Jesuit schools he attended. At his mother's advice he enrolled in medical school at the University of Edinburgh at age 17. He was intrigued by the scientific method and rationalism, and he was especially taken by one of his professors, Dr. Joseph Bell. To arrive at diagnoses the professor relied on observation and deductive reasoning—tools that would come to be wielded by Doyle's most famous literary creation, Sherlock Holmes.

While he was in medical school Doyle published his first short story, "The Mystery of Sasassa Valley." Influenced by Edgar Allen Poe, the tale reflected his interest in thrillers. After a series of adventures took him around the world, he moved to Portsmouth and set up his medical practice. In 1885 he married

Louise Hawkins; they had two children. In 1888 he published his first Sherlock Holmes novel, *A Study in Scarlet*, in the literary magazine *Beeton's Christmas Annual*. Between 1891 and 1893 he published new Sherlock Holmes stories in *The Strand Magazine*. (*The Adventures of Sherlock Holmes* is a collection of the first 12 stories.) He grew weary of his famous character, however, and in 1893 he killed off Holmes in the story "The Final Problem." Doyle's fan base was so immense and so captivated by his stories that an estimated 20,000 readers cancelled their subscriptions to *The Strand* in protest over Holmes's "death." The public outcry was so great, in fact, he resurrected the detective in a 1903 story.

Doyle's reason-wielding, crime-fighting sleuth has come to be one of the most well-known and influential figures in literary and pop culture history. From detective Sam Spade in Dashiell Hammett's 1930 novel *The Maltese Falcon* to the *CSI* television franchise, the clue-hunting detective character has remained a permanent fixture in storytelling. Despite the many talented detectives he inspired, Holmes has not been eclipsed; the immense worldwide popularity of *Sherlock*, the British TV series launched in 2010, which recast Holmes's adventures in modern London, demonstrates his continued appeal. Holmes's influence on literature is so monumental that a literary journal dedicated exclusively to Sherlock Holmes criticism, *The Baker Street Journal*, was created in 1946 and is still around today.

Many commentators have even credited Sherlock Holmes with contributing to the development of crime forensics. His intelligence-gathering techniques, such as analyzing fingerprints, blood, secret codes, footprints, and other physical clues, as well as his use of chemistry, directly influenced modern-day crime solving. The 2013 work *The Scientific Sherlock Holmes: Cracking the Case with Science and Forensics*, written by Missouri State University chemistry professor James O'Brien, devoted an entire book to this topic.

In addition to mysteries Doyle wrote essays, historical romances, plays, and more. He was a bona fide literary superstar, admired worldwide, and he visited the United States and other foreign lands on speaking tours. In 1906 Louise died after a years-long battle with tuberculosis, and Doyle remarried Jean Leckie, a beautiful and aristocratic young woman with whom he had been having an affair; they had three children.

Toward the end of his life Doyle became fascinated with "spiritualism," an occult movement that believed one could communicate with the dead. He developed a serious heart condition and, despite doctors' warnings, traveled around the world to promote spiritualism. On a tour in 1929, his heart pains became so severe that he had to return home, where he remained mostly restricted to bed until his death on July 7, 1930.

Characters

Sherlock Holmes

Sherlock Holmes is a private investigator who works from his home on Baker Street in central London. A devoted pupil of crime studies, he is a zealous believer in the powers of observation and deductive reasoning. Holmes is typically unflappable and reserved, but on occasion he exposes a passionate, creative side. He has no interest in being a part of London society; apart from his relationship with Dr. John Watson, he is something of a loner. He has a renowned reputation, and has been commissioned to tackle cases all over the world.

Dr. John Watson

Dr. John Watson is Sherlock Holmes's best friend and frequent sidekick. His medical practice isn't very busy, which allows him time to tag along with Holmes during his various crime-solving adventures. Watson is good-natured and smart, but he (like many others) frequently misses clues that are easily detectable to Sherlock Holmes.

Irene Adler

Though she was born in the United States, Irene Adler's opera career has taken her around Europe, where she meets the King of Bohemia and begins a romantic relationship with him. Her anger at the king causes her to make a rash decision, but she is otherwise poised and shrewd—so much so, in fact, she gets the better of Holmes and the king when they come looking for the photos she holds of her ex-lover.

Lestrade

Lestrade is a long-serving investigator at Scotland Yard, the police force of the city of London, but his main role is foil to Sherlock Holmes, who frequently exposes his incompetence. He represents the establishment, and accordingly he is conventional in every way—including his thinking. He has a prominent role in "The Boscombe Valley Mystery" and "The Adventure of the Noble Bachelor."

Character Map

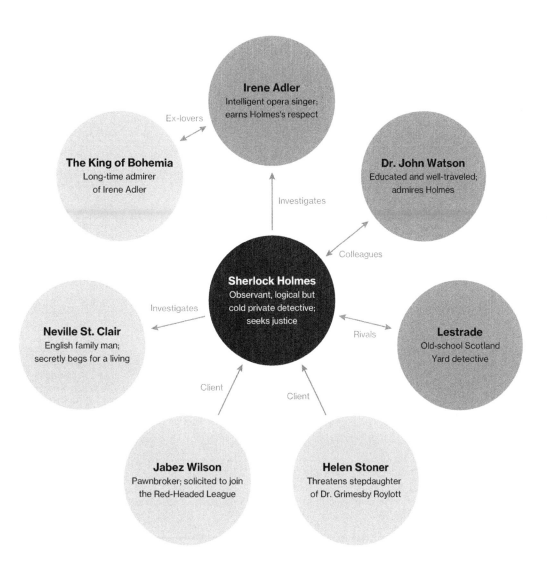

● Main Character

● Other Major Character

● Minor Character

Course Hero

Full Character List

Character	Description
Sherlock Holmes	Sherlock Holmes is a private investigator based in London who solves all kinds of crimes and mysteries by acting as a consultant to stumped authorities.
Dr. John Watson	London physician Dr. John Watson is a crime-solving collaborator and confidant of Sherlock Holmes.
Irene Adler	Irene Adler is a New Jersey-born opera singer and a former lover of the King of Bohemia; she appears in "A Scandal in Bohemia."
Lestrade	Lestrade is a veteran Scotland Yard detective.
Henry Baker	Henry Baker is an older British gentleman who loses his hat and his goose after he is attacked by a gang; he appears in "The Adventure of the Blue Carbuncle."
Inspector Bradstreet	Inspector Bradstreet is the London detective who watches over the beggar Hugh Boone (later revealed to be Neville St. Clair) in jail; he appears in "The Man with the Twisted Lip."
Breckenridge	Breckenridge runs the stall at the Covent Garden market, and he unwittingly sells the goose with the Countess's blue carbuncle in its crop to the Alpha Inn; he appears in "The Adventure of the Blue Carbuncle."
Sir George Burnwell	Sir George Burnwell is the rake and career criminal who seduces Mary Holder into stealing the Beryl Coronet; he appears in "The Adventure of the Beryl Coronet."
John Clay	John Clay is the well-known criminal who, under the alias Vincent Spaulding, concocts the scheme of the Red-Headed League in order to get Jabez Wilson out of his house; he appears in "The Red-Headed League."
Catherine Cusack	Catherine Cusack is the Countess of Morcar's maid and James Ryder's co-conspirator in the theft of the countess's blue carbuncle; she appears in "The Adventure of the Blue Carbuncle."
Aloysius Doran	Aloysius Doran, the father of Hatty Doran, is an extremely wealthy American who made his money mining gold; he appears in "The Adventure of the Noble Bachelor."
Hatty Doran	Hatty Doran is the American-born 20-year-old who disappeared after her marriage to Lord St. Simon; she appears in "The Adventure of the Noble Bachelor."
Mr. Fowler	Mr. Fowler is Alice Rucastle's love interest and eventually her husband; he helps her escape from captivity at Copper Beeches in "The Adventure of the Copper Beeches."
Victor Hatherley	Victor Hatherley is the hydraulic engineer who is hired to service a hydraulic press used by a counterfeiting gang; he loses his thumb during his escape from the gang; he appears in "The Adventure of the Engineer's Thumb."
Alexander Holder	Alexander Holder is the wealthy London banker who hires Holmes to find the missing section of the Beryl Coronet, which was stolen from his room; he appears in "The Adventure of the Beryl Coronet."
Arthur Holder	Arthur Holder is Alexander Holder's hedonistic son; he is falsely accused of stealing the missing fragment of the Beryl Coronet; he appears in "The Adventure of the Beryl Coronet."

Mary Holder	Mary Holder, Alexander Holder's beloved niece, steals the Beryl Coronet from his dressing room while he is sleeping; she appears in "The Adventure of the Beryl Coronet."
John Horner	John Horner is the plumber accused of stealing the Countess of Morcar's blue carbuncle after he services her room at the Hotel Cosmopolitan; he appears in "The Adventure of the Blue Carbuncle."
Miss Violet Hunter	Miss Violet Hunter is the governess who asks Sherlock Holmes to help her figure out the mystery at Copper Beeches; she appears in "The Adventure of the Copper Beeches."
Peter Jones	Peter Jones is a Scotland Yard policeman who accompanies Sherlock Holmes and Dr. John Watson to their confrontation with the criminal John Clay; he appears in "The Red-Headed League."
The King of Bohemia	The King of Bohemia is an ex-lover of Irene Adler's and hires Holmes to get back incriminating photos of the two of them together; he appears in "A Scandal in Bohemia."
The lascar	The lascar is a sailor of Asian origin who manages the London opium den Bar of Gold; he appears in "The Man with the Twisted Lip."
Charles McCarthy	Charles McCarthy is the Australian who blackmails John Turner; he lives on the Turner property, along with his son, for free; he appears in "The Boscombe Valley Mystery."
James McCarthy	James McCarthy, the son of Charles McCarthy, is accused of murdering his father; he appears in "The Boscombe Valley Mystery."
Mr. Merryweather	Mr. Merryweather is the director of the bank behind Jabez Wilson's pawnshop; he appears in "The Red-Headed League."
Flora Millar	Flora Millar is a former danseuse and ex-lover of Lord St. Simon; she appears in "The Adventure of the Noble Bachelor."
Frank Moulton	Frank Moulton is Hatty Doran's first husband; he appears in "The Adventure of the Noble Bachelor."
Maggie Oakshott	Maggie Oakshott is James Ryder's sister and the woman who raised the geese Ryder used to hide the blue carbuncle in; she appears in "The Adventure of the Blue Carbuncle."
Elias Openshaw	Elias Openshaw is murdered by the Ku Klux Klan because he tries to defy them after he returns to Horsham, the English town where he is from; he appears in "The Five Orange Pips."
John Openshaw	John Openshaw is the nephew of former K.K.K. affiliate Elias Openshaw; he is murdered by the group in retaliation against his uncle; he appears in Chapter 5, "The Five Orange Pips."
Joseph Openshaw	Joseph Openshaw, the father of John Openshaw and the brother of Elias Openshaw, is murdered by the K.K.K. in retaliation against his brother; he appears in "The Five Orange Pips."
Commissionaire Peterson	Commissionaire Peterson breaks up the assault on Henry Baker and brings the goose Baker leaves at the scene to Holmes; he appears in "The Adventure of the Blue Carbuncle."
Dr. Grimesby Roylott	Roylott is the troubled heir to one of Britain's most illustrious Saxon families and the stepfather to Helen Stoner and her deceased sister Julie; he appears in "The Adventure of the Speckled Band."

Alice Rucastle	Alice Rucastle, Mr. Rucastle's daughter from his first marriage, is the person locked in a room in the restricted wing of Copper Beeches; she appears in "The Adventure of the Copper Beeches."
Mr. Rucastle	Mr. Rucastle tricks Miss Violet Hunter into impersonating his imprisoned daughter, Alice Rucastle, under the pretext of serving as governess for Rucastle's six-year-old boy; he appears in "The Adventure of the Copper Beeches."
Mrs. Rucastle	Mrs. Rucastle, who is in her early 30s, is the stepmother to Alice Rucastle; she appears in "The Adventure of the Copper Beeches."
James Ryder	James Ryder is the hotel attendant at the Hotel Cosmopolitan who plots the theft of the Countess of Morcar's blue carbuncle; he appears in "The Adventure of the Blue Carbuncle."
The German counterfeiter	Using the alias Colonel Lysander Stark, the German counterfeiter recruits Victor Hatherley to fix the malfunctioning hydraulic press he has been using to make fake coins; his real name is Fritz. He appears in "The Adventure of the Engineer's Thumb."
Mrs. St. Clair	Mrs. St. Clair hires Sherlock Holmes to find her missing husband, Neville St. Clair; she appears in "The Man with the Twisted Lip."
Neville St. Clair	Neville St. Clair is the affluent suburban man who secretly makes his (considerable) living as a beggar named Hugh Boone; he appears in "The Man with the Twisted Lip."
Helen Stoner	Helen Stoner has been living under the strict guardianship of her stepfather, Grimesby Roylott, in his crumbling family mansion in Stoke Moran; she appears in "The Adventure of the Speckled Band."

Julia Stoner	Julia Stoner, the twin sister of Helen Stoner, died mysteriously in her room at the Roylott family mansion; she appears in "The Adventure of the Speckled Band."
Lord St. Simon	Lord St. Simon is the British aristocrat who hires Holmes to find his wife, the former Hatty Doran, who disappeared shortly after their wedding; he appears in "The Adventure of the Noble Bachelor."
Mary Sutherland	Mary Sutherland is the young typist who is duped out of her inheritance by her stepfather, James Windibank; she appears in "A Case of Identity."
Mr. Toller	Mr. Toller is a drunken house servant at Copper Beeches; he appears in "The Adventure of the Copper Beeches.
Mrs. Toller	Mrs. Toller is a servant at Copper Beeches who helps arrange Alice Rucastle's freedom; she appears in "The Adventure of the Copper Beeches."
Alice Turner	Alice Turner is the daughter of John Turner and the love interest of James McCarthy; she appears in "The Boscombe Valley Mystery."
John Turner	John Turner is a wealthy English landholder and the murderer of Charles McCarthy; he appears in "The Boscombe Valley Mystery."
Isa Whitney	A family friend of Dr. John Watson and his wife, Isa Whitney is an opium addict; he appears in "The Man with the Twisted Lip."
Jabez Wilson	Jabez Wilson is a middle-aged pawnbroker who is recruited to join the Red-Headed League; he appears in "The Red-Headed League."

James Windibank	James Windibank is the young stepfather of Mary Sutherland; along with her mother he concocts an elaborate ruse to access Sutherland's inheritance, while at the same time wooing her in disguise under the alias Hosmer Angel; he appears in "A Case of Identity."
Young German woman	The young German woman is part of Colonel Lysander Stark's counterfeiting operation, although she tries to help Victor Hatherley escape when Stark tries to kill him; she appears in "The Adventure of the Engineer's Thumb."

〽 Plot Summary

The appeal of Arthur Conan Doyle's Sherlock Holmes stories comes from their skillful blend of intelligence and entertainment. The stories challenge readers to hunt for clues and develop their own hypotheses as each narrative unfolds, but in the time between the crime and the resolution, readers come across all sorts of enchantingly drawn characters. The long friendship between Sherlock Holmes and Dr. John Watson is particularly remarkable and gives each story a sense of continuity. The men spend much time making witty banter, but their connection is heartfelt and offers readers an affirming antidote to the double-crossing that Holmes so frequently encounters in his investigations. In *The Adventures of Sherlock Holmes* each story is self-contained, although certain characters appear in more than one story.

A Scandal in Bohemia

This short story is told in three chapters and features the reunion of Sherlock Holmes and Dr. Watson after a period of separation. The action revolves around the King of Bohemia. He is getting married, and he must recover compromising letters and a photo that are in the hands of an ex-lover, the enchanting opera singer Irene Adler. The intelligent and witty Adler, however, proves too elusive for the king and even for the great Holmes as she herself gets married and makes her escape with the photo—just in case she ever needs to use it in the future.

The Red-Headed League

A red-headed pawnbroker named Jabez Wilson is encouraged by his assistant, Vincent Spaulding, to join a secretive organization dedicated to honoring red-headed men. Wilson is chosen by the Red-Headed League to copy an encyclopedia by hand for four hours daily at a good rate of pay, with the stipulation that he not leave the office. After eight weeks, however, the office is closed suddenly, so Wilson comes to Sherlock Holmes to learn if he is the victim of a ruse. The organization turns out to be a sham concocted by Spaulding, who is actually a notorious criminal named John Clay. He needed Wilson to be away from the shop so he could build a tunnel from the basement to a nearby bank that he intended to rob.

A Case of Identity

A young woman named Mary Sutherland is tricked into keeping her inheritance under the control of her stepfather and mother in a cruel case of deception. Her controlling stepfather, James Windibank, disguises himself as a man named Hosmer Angel. Mary falls in love with this mysterious man and pledges to remain true to him no matter what. On the day they are supposed to be married, Angel disappears. When Sherlock Holmes figures out the scam, he doesn't have the heart to break it to the woman, but he threatens violence on Windibank and tells Dr. Holmes that he believes the man will soon turn to a life of crime.

The Boscombe Valley Mystery

Sherlock Holmes and Dr. Watson travel to Herefordshire to help Scotland Yard Inspector Lestrade solve a case brought to Holmes by a young woman named Alice Turner. The father of the man she loves has been murdered at Boscombe Pool, and his son has been accused and jailed for the crime. After visiting the crime scene and talking to the young man in prison, James McCarthy, Holmes knows who the murderer is and gives the inspector a description of him without revealing the man's name. Holmes then invites the killer, John Turner (Alice's father), to his hotel and gets a signed confession from the man. It turns out that Turner and the murdered Charles McCarthy, who both came from Australia, had ties based on a terrible secret from the past. Turner had been a notorious criminal in Australia, and McCarthy has been blackmailing him for years to keep the information secret. When he pushed the blackmail beyond monetary demands to the demand that Alice marry James, Turner snapped. However, he is very ill and only has a few months to live, so Holmes does not turn him over to Scotland Yard. Instead, at James's trial he establishes reasonable doubt and James is then free to marry Alice.

The Five Orange Pips

In a case involving the Ku Klux Klan, Sherlock Holmes becomes incensed by the crimes that occur and seeks revenge for them on his own. The case is brought to him by a young man named John Openshaw, who believes his family is cursed and is afraid he will be the third generation of men to be killed, since he has recently received the same strange letter that his grandfather and father received just before their "accidental" deaths. Each letter is marked KKK and contains five orange pips (seeds or pits) with instructions to put papers from a chest also marked KKK and kept in the Openshaw house "on the sundial." Holmes figures out that the papers most desired by the Ku Klux Klan are a register of all member names. He warns John Openshaw to practice extreme caution, but the man nevertheless dies overnight in a drowning accident. Holmes traces the letters to the captain of a ship that is en route to Savannah, Georgia. He alerts authorities there to arrest James Calhoun upon arrival, but it becomes unnecessary when the ship sinks in a storm and all aboard perish.

The Man with the Twisted Lip

In a strange case that moves from an opium den in London, to Kent, and then back to London, Sherlock Holmes discovers a startling secret that does not actually involve a crime. A woman from Kent named Mrs. St. Clair is seeking her missing husband, Neville, who has been presumed dead but has just written her a letter that proves he is alive. A well-known beggar in London, Hugh Boone, has been accused of his murder. Holmes figures out Boone is actually Neville St. Clair in disguise. He has been secretly making his living by begging, since he earns much more money at that than he ever did as a journalist.

The Adventure of the Blue Carbuncle

Set at Christmas time this case involves a countess, who is missing her huge blue diamond; a holiday goose; a battered hat; and Sherlock Holmes, who takes justice into his own hands. Holmes has been given a holiday goose and a hat by Commissionaire Peterson, who came by these items while breaking up a street scuffle and hopes the detective will return them to their rightful owner. Holmes keeps the hat but tells Peterson to cook the goose for holiday dinner before it spoils. In preparing the bird for cooking, Mrs. Peterson finds a big blue diamond in its throat, the precious Blue Carbuncle that the Countess of Morcar has reported missing from her hotel room. Following many clues, including the initials HB on the hat, Holmes determines the identity of the thief, a hotel employee named James Ryder. However, since the jewel is recovered, Holmes allows Ryder to flee, and without sufficient evidence to prove guilt another hotel employee wrongly accused of the theft is set free.

The Adventure of the Speckled Band

A very frightened young woman named Helen Stoner visits Sherlock Holmes, afraid for her life. She is about to be married but fears she will suffer the same fate as her twin sister who died mysteriously just before her own wedding. The death occurred at Stoke Moran, the mansion belonging to their stepfather Grimesby Roylott. He is a foul-tempered man who keeps exotic pets on the grounds of the crumbling mansion and receives quite a bit of money from Helen's mother's estate as long as Helen remains single. Helen tells Holmes of the circumstances surrounding her sister's death, including strange whistling sounds heard in her bedroom on the nights leading up to it and her remark while dying that it was "the speckled band." For the past few nights, Helen has been hearing whistling noises in her bedroom, the same room her twin sister once occupied. Holmes and Dr. Watson visit Stoke Moran, and after careful investigation Holmes determines that they should return to spend the night in Helen's room while she sleeps elsewhere. That night, shortly after Holmes beats on the walls of the room with his cane, a scream comes from

Grimesby Roylott's neighboring room. He is found dead from the bite of an Indian swamp adder, a snake that he has been sending into Helen's room to kill her and calling back with a whistle as morning approaches.

The Adventure of the Engineer's Thumb

Dr. Watson brings a young engineer named Victor Hatherley to Sherlock Holmes after treating him for the loss of a thumb, which was chopped off as Hatherley escaped a near-death experience. The previous night, Hatherley was taken to a location hidden from him to work on a hydraulic press that he can tell has been used to press metal. After Hatherley diagnoses the problem and tells the owner how to repair it, the owner and his partner try to kill him. The machine has been used to produce counterfeit coins, and they are afraid Hatherley will figure that out and turn them in. After asking a few questions, doing some research, and enlisting the help of Scotland Yard, Holmes is able to locate the mansion where the press is; the house has been set ablaze. However, the criminals are never caught.

The Adventure of the Noble Bachelor

In a case that turns out to be something of a love triangle, Sherlock Holmes is contacted by the esteemed Lord St. Simon to find his wife, who went missing at their wedding breakfast. Hatty Doran, whom St. Simon has just married, is an American millionaire's daughter, and the lord is in love both with her and with the money she brings to the marriage. However, that money is not to be his, as Holmes discovers Hatty is already married—to a man presumed dead who has just reappeared in her life.

The Adventure of the Beryl Coronet

A prominent banker named Alexander Holder approaches Sherlock Holmes with a sensitive case that could ruin his reputation and tear apart his family. As collateral for a very large loan, he has accepted a beryl coronet, a type of crown worn by nobles that is set with 39 precious gems. Thinking it is safer to keep it in his own home for the short duration of the loan, Holder locks the coronet in a bureau in his dressing room, telling only his son, Arthur, and his niece, Mary—both of whom live with him. That night he hears someone in his dressing room and rushes in to find Arthur holding the coronet, which is missing three of the stones. As Arthur swears his innocence, Mary enters the dressing room and faints upon seeing what is going on. Holder believes Arthur is guilty and has sold the stones to pay for his gambling habit. Mary, however, thinks the guilt lies with a new servant girl named Lucy Parr. Holmes solves the case overnight and goes to Holder's home the next morning for a check he can use to purchase the missing stones. When he learns that Mary is missing, he is not surprised and explains that she and the man she loves—a frequent visitor to the Holmes house—are the culprits. Arthur knew the two stole the crown, and in fact wrestled it away from the man, causing the stones to fall off in the street outside the house. But he protected Mary because he is deeply in love with her. Holmes then takes the check to buy the stones from a pawnbroker, keeping what is left over as his fee and declining Holder's request to try to find Mary.

The Adventure of the Copper Beeches

When young Violet Hunter first comes to Sherlock Holmes to seek his advice, she does not take it. She has been offered a high-paying job as a governess to the Rucastle family, who live on an estate called the Copper Beeches in Hampshire. The strange stipulations of the job are what cause her to wonder if she should accept the position, but although Holmes warns her of danger she does ultimately say yes. Holmes encourages her to contact him should the situation present problems. Sure enough, Violet sends him a late-night telegram two weeks later, and he and Dr. Watson rush to her aid.

Violet has been forced to cut her hair short and is often told to sit in a certain chair with her back to the window, wearing a blue dress given to her by her employers. Using a mirror, she has seen a young man on the grounds gazing at the window. She has also discovered a locked room where she is convinced someone lives. Holmes soon solves the mystery. The person locked in the room is Alice Rucastle, Mr. Rucastle's daughter by his first wife. The man gazing at the window is Alice's fiance, Mr. Fowler. The Rucastles are having Violet pose as Alice to back up the story they have told him that he is no longer welcome at Copper Beeches. Mr. Rucastle does not want her to marry because he will lose access to the fortune her mother left her. Just as Holmes reaches these conclusions, however, a servant at Copper Beeches has aided Alice in escaping to join her fiance, so the story has a happy ending.

⊙ Story Summaries

A Scandal in Bohemia

Summary

Chapter 1

An unnamed narrator describes, in first-person, Sherlock Holmes's obsession with a woman named Irene Adler. After the narrator's description of Adler, he explains he hasn't seen Holmes in some time. The narrator has been occupied with his new wife and his home, and Holmes has either been either holed up in his home on Baker Street, in London, studying crime-solving techniques or out solving crimes in different locales In Europe and Asia.

The narrator then describes a recent encounter he had with Holmes. On an evening in March 1888, while he is travelling home after visiting a patient, the narrator (a doctor, we learn) passes Holmes's house and feels compelled to pay his old friend a visit. When the narrator enters the house, Holmes's greeting reveals his name: Watson. Holmes immediately makes a number of observations about Dr. Watson: he has returned to practicing medicine, he has been walking in the rain recently, and his servant girl is doing a poor job. Watson is astounded by Holmes's assertions, which are all correct, and asks him to explain how he came to them. Holmes laughs, and then explains he simply focused on small but revealing details in Watson's presentation such as: a noticeable scar on Watson's shoe, which indicates that mud was scraped off it (presumably by an incompetent servant); and a mark of nitrate of silver on Watson's finger, indicating his work in medicine. "I see it, I deduce it," he says.

Holmes then asks Watson to look over a letter he's been examining. The letter, which was written on expensive notepaper, says at a quarter to eight this evening, a "gentleman" will pay a visit to Holmes's residence to discuss something important. As well he may be wearing a mask. Holmes and Watson scrutinize the notepaper. They quickly deduce the letter was written by a wealthy Bohemian (someone from the German-speaking central European country). Their predictions are confirmed after the letter writer arrives at Holmes's house.

The masked guest is a towering hulk of a man. At first he claims he is the representative of the House of Ormstein, a royal Bohemian dynasty, but after Holmes sees through his meager disguise he confesses he is indeed the King of Bohemia. He explains his predicament: Five years ago, while he was in Warsaw, he had a relationship with an "adventuress" named Irene Adler. At mention of her name Holmes instructs Watson to find Adler's file in his archives, a comprehensive record of "men and things" the detective keeps. Her file reveals she is a retired American opera singer who was living in London (and had once lived in Warsaw). The king confirms these details, and explains he had sent Adler "some compromising letters" and a photo of the two of them together.

The king explains none of his attempts to silence her have been successful; he has tried to pay her off, and he even had her house burglarized and her luggage confiscated. He is supposed to announce his engagement to the King of Sweden's daughter in three days, but Adler has threatened to send the photo to her family on the day the engagement is announced. Holmes asks the king for Adler's address in London, and instructs Watson to return to his house at three o'clock the next day.

Chapter 2

Watson returns on time, but Holmes isn't there. Soon, however, he arrives home—wearing the disguise of a shabby horse groom. He explains to Watson his disguise enabled him to get information about Adler from her stable staff and to survey her homestead without suspicion. He learned she's frequently visited by an attractive lawyer named Godfrey Norton, which concerns him. If Norton is her lawyer or friend, she may have given him the photo or mentioned it to him; if she's his mistress, however, it's unlikely Norton would know about it. While Holmes was mulling this he saw Adler and Norton race off for the Church of St. Monica in separate carriages. He followed in his own carriage. When he got to church he saw they were at the altar, and after a short time spying he was dragged to the altar to be a witness to their marriage. Holmes worried this meant they would flee together from London (along with the photo), and was relieved when they departed the church in separate carriages. He returned to his house to meet Watson.

Holmes asks if Watson will act as an accomplice while he makes his way into Adler's house to find the location of the photo. Watson cheerfully agrees, despite Holmes's warning that their caper is illegal and may lead to arrest. Holmes explains he will find a way to get into the house. A few minutes after he's inside, the sitting-room window will be opened; at Holmes's signal, Watson is to throw a smoke rocket into the room and yell "fire!"

That evening the duo goes to Adler's house; Holmes is disguised as a clergyman. As Adler's carriage arrives a fight breaks out among the "loafing men" standing nearby and her security personnel. Holmes rushes toward the scene to assist Adler, but when he enters in the fray he's bloodied and knocked down. He's escorted into Adler's sitting room to recover, and after a few minutes one of Adler's maids rushes to open the window and give the bruised clergyman some air. As instructed Watson throws the rocket through the window and yells "fire," setting off a commotion in the house.

Watson and Holmes regroup later outside the house, and Holmes explains he didn't retrieve the photo, but he did identify its location: a recess near the bell pull. Exactly as Holmes had planned, the thought of losing such a precious item to a fire spurred Adler to reach for the photo. Holmes's announcement that the fire was a false alarm, however, spurred her to return the photo to the recess. Holmes also explains that the fighting mob in front of Adler's carriage had been organized by him, and the "blood" on his face was simply red paint. Holmes says he, Watson, and the king should return to the house at eight o'clock the following morning to retrieve the photo, reasoning Adler will not yet be up. As Holmes and Watson reach Holmes's house, a young man walking by wishes Holmes a good night and then disappears.

Chapter 3

The trio arrives at Adler's house the next morning. The king, who has never lost interest in Adler, sulks when Holmes informs him she is now married. The three men walk up to Adler's house, and are met by one of her servants. They are taken aback when the servant addresses Holmes by his name. She informs them Adler and Norton left England on a 5:15 a.m. train. Holmes rushes toward the recess, and pulls out a photo of Adler (by herself) and a letter addressed to him. The letter explains Adler had been notified a few months ago that "the celebrated Sherlock Holmes" may be hired by the king. Still,

she didn't realize she was being followed by Sherlock Holmes until the false alarm. After realizing she'd been the target of Holmes, she disguised herself as a youth and followed the "clergyman" to his home and confirmed his true identity. She says the king need not worry; she is now a happily married woman, and has no interest in exposing their former relationship. However, she is holding on to the photo to protect herself from any future harm. After reading the letter, the king moons over her yet again, and complains she cannot be his queen. He thanks Holmes for resolving the matter. Holmes asks the king if he may keep Adler's photo. The king agrees.

Analysis

This first story introduces readers to the collection's two main characters, the crime-solving investigator Sherlock Holmes and his friend (and frequent accomplice) Dr. Watson. The opening anecdote, which describes Holmes's mysterious relationship to the woman named Irene Adler, reveals much about Sherlock Holmes's personality and beliefs.

The specific reason this woman has so captured Holmes's imagination is only alluded to, but it's clear her intense effect on him is atypical. As "the most perfect reasoning and observing machine that the world has seen," Holmes disdains emotional responses such as passion and love, because "such intrusions into his own delicate and finely adjusted temperament" could distract him from his mission and "throw a doubt upon all his mental results," Watson explains. Nonetheless, it is clear Adler has unsettled Holmes, machine or not. Holmes refers to Adler simply as "the woman," further clarification being unnecessary.

After commenting on Holmes's fixation on Adler, Watson, who is narrating the story, moves on to profiling Holmes himself, whom he describes as something of a loner and a workaholic; when he's not traveling around the world solving crimes, he likes to hole up at his home on Baker Street and bury himself in his books. He "loathes" society, Watson tells us—and frequently uses cocaine. Temperamentally, Holmes is extremely composed and unemotional; when Watson arrives to his house, he muses, Holmes "was glad, I think, to see me." His disposition reflects his world view, which is guided by logic and reasoning. He is all head, and very little heart (with exceptions)—and thus has little interest in small talk, niceties, or similar exchanges that don't have a utilitarian purpose. Accordingly, It's no wonder he's not very interested in social functions.

Before the king interrupts their meeting, Holmes explains to Watson his shortcomings in perception. "You see, but you do not observe," he tells Watson. "The distinction is clear." Holmes has trained himself to look at objects and people with fresh eyes and enormous concentration—even mundane things like the number of steps in his house (17, to be precise). This process has enabled him to wring clues out of everyday things most people overlook. He is such an astute clue-catcher because his reasoning depends on it; his deductions—and ultimately, conclusions—are only as good as his information. Thus his remarkable power of observation is a crucial tool for intelligence gathering.

Holmes's confident, if not superior, view of his abilities may explain his infatuation with Irene Adler. She not only outsmarted Sherlock Holmes, the renowned crime-solver and master of disguise, but she challenged his ideas—and surely, many readers' ideas—of what a woman is capable of. When Adler's servant greets Holmes by his name after the trio arrives at the Adler residence, the typically calm investigator gets a "questioning" and "rather startled" look on his face. Her cleverness, it seems, enchants him. (Likewise, the King of Bohemia grows even more enamored of her; "what a woman—oh, what a woman!" he exclaims after reading her letter.)

It's interesting that this story—the very first Sherlock Holmes tale Doyle published, no less—ends in failure. It may seem strange and even a little risky to introduce a new fictional character who fails, but this demonstrates Doyle's originality and, possibly, a subversion of reader expectations. Even great men aren't always great, Doyle seems to be telling the reader. Paradoxically, Holmes's very failure makes him a more sympathetic character.

The Red-Headed League

Summary

One fall day Dr. Watson stops by Sherlock Holmes's house to say hello, and he finds Holmes deep in conversation with a red-headed London pawnbroker named Jabez Wilson. At Holmes's request Wilson begins explaining to Dr. Watson the strange series of events that spurred his visit.

Two months earlier, Wilson's assistant, Vincent Spaulding, alerted him to a strange advertisement in *The Morning Chronicle* newspaper. The ad claimed to be placed by an American organization called "the Red-Headed League," and it was offering to pay a red-headed London man £4 a week in exchange for doing a few hours of busy work each day. Spaulding, who worked competently for half the typical wages of his position, expressed excitement at the opportunity for Wilson. He asked, incredulously, if Wilson had "never heard of the League of the Red-headed men?" After further convincing by Spaulding, Wilson applied for the position in person the following Monday, accompanied by his assistant. The interview was run by a representative of the League named Duncan Ross. Ross pulled Wilson's red hair to make sure it was real, and then outlined the parameters of the position: Wilson was to copy out the *Encyclopaedia Britannica* by hand between the hours of ten and two o'clock, each day of the week. He could not leave the building for any reason between these hours, but if he complied he would be given the weekly allowance of £4. Given the seeming ease of the task, he immediately accepted the position and agreed to start the next day.

Despite his apprehension that the arrangement was too good to be true, his first day of "work" went exactly as promised, and he returned to the league office every workday for eight weeks. After the end of the eighth week, however, he arrived at work and found the door of his office locked and a note on the door declaring the league had been dissolved. Confused by the unexpected closure, Wilson tracked down the landlord of the building. He told Wilson the office's tenant was a solicitor named William Morris, not Duncan Ross, and he recently moved out. Wilson traveled to Morris's new office address (which Morris gave to the landlord), but it turned out to be the address for a prosthetics company that had never heard of Morris or Ross. Confounded by the strange series of events and worried he had been tricked, Wilson contacted Sherlock Holmes.

Holmes begins his investigation by asking Wilson about his assistant, Vincent Spaulding. He learns Wilson hired Spaulding from a pool of applicants because he was competent and considerably cheaper than the rest of the group. Holmes learns Spaulding is short, strong, around 30, and has pierced ears—a fact that particularly intrigues the investigator. Holmes takes a 50-minute smoke break—this is a "three pipe problem," he asserts—and then he and Watson take the underground (subway) to scope out the area around Wilson's pawnshop, Coburg Square. That afternoon they survey the area around the shop and then knock on the door. For seemingly unclear reasons, Holmes beats the ground around the house with a stick. A young man (presumably Spaulding) opens the door, and Holmes asks him for directions, noticing the worn-out knees of his trousers. Holmes makes a mental note of all of the businesses that surround Wilson's shop (including a bank), and then they attend a performance of Sarasate (a Spanish violinist) at a nearby church.

After the performance Holmes tells Watson, with some graveness, to meet him at Baker Street at ten o'clock that evening. In the meantime, Holmes says, he must further explore Coburg Square. When Watson arrives to Holmes's house he is joined by two other men, a Scotland Yard policeman named Peter Jones and a bank director named Mr. Merryweather. Jones explains they are closing in on an infamous criminal named John Clay, a "thief, smasher, and forger" who has eluded capture. The grandson of a Duke and an Oxford graduate, he has been involved in multiple high-profile scams over the years. The group of men travel to a street close to Coburg Square, and led by Merryweather travel through back alleys and stairs until they arrive at the pitch-black vault of the very bank Holmes had identified earlier in the day. There are a number of boxes and crates in the vault; Merryweather explains they are holding £30,000 in gold bullion loaned from the Bank of France. After closely examining the floor, Holmes warns that John Clay and his associates will be arriving shortly—after Wilson has gone to bed—and directs the men to hide in the dark. As predicted after a little more than an hour the floor of the vault opens and Clay (Vincent Spaulding) emerges. Holmes accosts him, complimenting the plotter for the creativity of the Red-Headed League as Jones puts him in handcuffs. Ever the snob, Clay insists the policeman defer to his high breeding and call him "sir."

Back at Baker Street later that night, Holmes explains to Watson how he deduced the plot. First, the idea of a "league" of red-headed men was so preposterous (and hilarious) it convinced him something sketchy must be afoot. Indeed, the fact that league "duties" would keep Wilson out of his shop each day, while his clever—and significantly underpaid—assistant is left in charge of the pawnshop convinced Holmes that Clay (Spaulding) must be involved. No doubt his photography "hobby" coupled with his frequent visits to Wilson's cellar under the guise of developing his pictures means he was doing something in the cellar. As well, the wear in the knees of Jones's pants suggested he had been spending

a lot of time on the ground. Last, Holmes explains his pavement-beating was to figure out what direction Wilson's cellar led toward. It led toward the back—the direction of the bank. Clay had been building a secret tunnel while Wilson was at work. Because "the league" had just notified Wilson of its cancellation, Holmes knew he had to act quickly, lest Clay and his accomplice escape with the gold.

Analysis

"The Red-Headed League" is an original mystery and one of the most well-known Sherlock Holmes stories. It includes the classic display of deductive reasoning Sherlock Holmes is known for. For example, after spending very little time with Wilson, Holmes (accurately) observes Wilson "has at some time done manual labour, that he takes snuff, that he is a Freemason, that he has been in China, and that he has done a considerable amount of writing lately." However, the absurd premise elevates the tale from mere mystery to highbrow comedy. "Duo of enterprising bank vault robbers setting up a fake society dedicated to honoring the world's redheaded men" isn't exactly a plot cliché.

What gives the ruse even more comic power is that the recipient of this honor is Jabez Wilson, a modest pawnbroker from a drab area of London. Watson observes—not without a measure of condescension—that Wilson "bore every mark of being an average commonplace British tradesman, obese, pompous, and slow." The only thing exceptional about Wilson was that he was a "blazing redhead," he adds. The spectacle of such a man being caught up in such a group brings Holmes and Watson nearly to tears with laughter. When Wilson shows them the note on his door informing him the league had been dissolved, Watson says, "Sherlock Holmes and I surveyed this curt announcement and the rueful face behind it, until the comical side of the affair so completely overtopped every other consideration that we both burst out into a roar of laughter."

The story touches on social class. Watson is a bit snooty in his description of Wilson, but the bank-vault robber, John Clay, is a fully unrepentant snob who feels superior even as he's being arrested for committing a crime. When the policeman, Jones, puts him in cuffs, Clay responds, "I beg that you will not touch me with your filthy hands ... Have the goodness, also, when you address me always to say 'sir' and 'please.'" The policeman plays along sarcastically, directing him to move along upstairs "where we can get a cab to carry Your Highness to the police station." The entire scene is merely a cherry on top of a story that's already preposterous enough.

The music scene offers a rare moment of contemplation in an otherwise straightforward and expertly plotted farce. During the Sarasate concert Holmes (who is a musician himself) seems transformed into another person. He is happily immersed in the music, even waving his fingers along with the violin. While he watches his friend, Watson thinks about human nature. He observes that Holmes's "languid, dreamy eyes" during the concert so starkly contrast "those of Holmes, the sleuth-hound, Holmes the relentless, keen-witted, ready-handed criminal agent." On occasion Holmes has a "poetic and contemplative" side, but Watson concludes his "extreme exactness" and faith in the power of deduction is Holmes's way of counterbalancing this more sensitive side. Watson's analysis suggests the debate between romanticism and realism. Violin-enthusiast Holmes—creative, passionate, "dreamy"—is romantic, while pipe-smoking Holmes, with his absolute embrace of reason, is a firm realist.

A Case of Identity

Summary

A young woman named Miss Mary Sutherland visits Holmes on Baker Street. Before her visit the detective had been discussing the nature of crime with Dr. Watson, arguing "life is infinitely stranger than anything the mind of man could invent." Sutherland was clearly in a hurry to get to Holmes's place: she explains she stormed out of her house to get away from her stepfather, James Windibank. Windibank has completely refused to help her in her quest: to find out what happened to a man named Hosmer Angel. She explains her father recently died, leaving his successful plumbing business in the hands of her mother. Much to Sutherland's alarm, she quickly married Mr. Windibank, who is only five years older than Sutherland. After pressure from Windibank, Sutherland's mother sold the plumbing business—albeit for a much lower price than Sutherland's father would have fetched. In addition Sutherland receives a yearly payment of £100 from a trust account set up by a deceased uncle in New Zealand. She forfeits most of this money to her mother and stepfather (with whom she lives), but with the remainder, in addition to the money she makes from

typing, she has a tidy income.

Sutherland explains she met Hosmer Angel at a gasfitters' ball. Windibank is fiercely controlling and had forbidden her from going to the event, but when he was supposed to be away in France on business she attended the ball with her mother. She hit it off with Angel, and over the next few days he called on her. The pair had taken walks together on two separate occasions before Windibank returned from France and put an end to the relationship. On their very first walk, however, Hosmer proposed to Sutherland, and she accepted, though she knew so little about him other than the fact that he worked as a cashier at some sort of office on Leadenhall Street in London. After Windibank forbade their seeing each other, the pair communicated by letter. Hosmer sent letters written by typewriter but asked that Sutherland send him handwritten notes. He also instructed her to send her letters to the post office on Leadenhall Street, so as not to draw his coworkers' attention to the courtship. A week later Windibank took off for France again, and Angel stopped by Sutherland's house. He asked Sutherland to marry him before her stepfather returned, and made her swear on a New Testament she "would always be true to him." With her mother's blessing—she told Sutherland she would deal with her stepfather and that she approved of Angel—Sutherland agreed.

On the morning of the wedding, a few days later, Angel arrived at Sutherland's house in a hansom cab. There wasn't enough room for him, Sutherland, and her mother in the cab, so he found a different cab to transport himself. When the cabs met up outside the church where the marriage was to take place, however, Angel was nowhere to be found. He hasn't been seen or heard from since. The previous Sunday, Sutherland placed a missing persons ad in a local paper describing Angel. Holmes asks Sutherland to leave her letters and ad with him and counsels her to leave the entire business behind. She thanks him and leaves, but not before saying she will keep her word to Angel and will wait for him.

Holmes discusses the case with Watson. As usual Watson has not detected a number of revealing clues Holmes has so easily assimilated. Believing he knows the answer to Angel's whereabouts, Holmes sends out two letters to confirm his suspicions: one to an unnamed London business, and one to James Windibank, asking him to visit Holmes the next evening at six o'clock. Windibank sends a letter back confirming he will visit Holmes. During their meeting Holmes accuses Windibank of disguising himself as Hosmer Angel in order to keep collecting Sutherland's trust payments and have access to her mother's money. He figured this out because Angel's description in the missing person advertisement includes common disguise articles: glasses, whiskers, and the like. In addition the letter Windibank sent to Holmes has the same typesetting errors as the letters "Angel" sent to Sutherland, meaning the same typewriter must have been used to author both letters. Windibank confesses to the crime, but insists it's not an actionable offense. Holmes agrees, and then throws him out.

Analysis

The conversation between Holmes and Watson at the beginning of the story foreshadows the crime in the story. During their discussion Holmes marvels at the sheer absurdity of most crimes, which, he argues, are far stranger than fiction, which is itself so often predictable and conventional. Holmes would appear to be correct, given that this story involves a plotting stepfather who marries into a well-to-do family and then disguises himself as a bridegroom for his own daughter-in-law only to leave her at the altar.

Mary Sutherland's ordeal clearly illustrates the subordinate position of women in Victorian society. Even though she's an adult, Sutherland's independence is completely subject to the whims of her parents—even her new stepfather, who is a mere five years older than she. His controlling behavior deeply affects her life; arguably his cruel plot to dupe her and take control of her money is simply an extreme version of his usual behavior. Even Sutherland's trust underscores her dependent status, because she is reliant on money from her uncle, an older man. Intentionally or not, the story calls attention to the injustice and unfairness many Victorian women faced in their society.

Like many other stories from *The Adventures of Sherlock Holmes*, disguise is a feature of this tale. It's interesting, however, that it's the culprit himself who dons a disguise in this story, not Sherlock Holmes. Windibank's deception adds a twist to the escapade, and shows Holmes must remain ever vigilant and open-minded in his crime-solving. Clearly the criminals and scofflaws he brings to justice are just as imaginative as the master detective himself.

The Boscombe Valley Mystery

Summary

While Watson is having breakfast with his wife, he receives a telegram from Holmes asking if he's free to accompany the detective on an investigation to the Boscombe Valley, a rural area in western England. Watson's wife encourages him to go, and after packing quickly Watson meets Holmes at Paddington Station, the central London train depot. During the ride Holmes catches Watson up on the details of the case and the people involved in it. He's been hired to investigate the murder of a man named Charles McCarthy, an Australian native who had been living on a farm owned by a wealthy local landholder named John Turner. During his youth Turner had lived in Australia—where he met McCarthy—and after amassing a small fortune he returned home to the Boscombe Valley. Both men were widowers with one child each; Turner has a daughter, Alice, and McCarthy had a son, James.

According to the police report and the coroner's examination, what happened was this: On the previous Monday, McCarthy was found dead by the Boscombe Pool, a small lake close to his rental property, Hatherley Farm. He had left Hatherley around three o'clock in the afternoon, telling his servant on the way out that he was going to meet up with someone. A gamekeeper witnessed McCarthy walking to Boscombe Pool; shortly after, however, he observed McCarthy's son (armed with a pistol) walking in the same direction. Another witness, a 14-year-old girl whose parent manages the Boscombe Valley estate, a local lodge, was in the woods near the lake when the two McCarthys met. She watched as they got into a violent argument, but after James McCarthy appeared to raise his hands to fight she ran off home. Very shortly after, James McCarthy came running toward the lodge shouting about his father's body. He did not have his gun on him, and his clothes had bloodstains. The lodge-keeper and others followed McCarthy to his father's body. McCarthy appeared to have been murdered by blunt-force trauma to the back of his head. As James McCarthy's gun was lying just a few feet away from the body, he was arrested and charged with murder.

In Watson's view the case is open-and-shut. The circumstantial evidence is completely damning, he says. Holmes, however, disagrees, arguing that circumstantial evidence "is a very tricky thing." At any rate he was contacted by Scotland Yard detective Lestrade to see if he can dig up any clues that might cast doubt on James McCarthy's guilt. Lestrade has been hired by Turner's daughter, Alice, a friend of McCarthy's who believes in his innocence.

Holmes and Watson continue discussing the case on the train. There seems to be one bright spot for McCarthy's defense: when he was arrested at Hatherley Farm, he did not plead innocence. Rather, he explained, "he was not surprised to hear it, and that it was no more than his desserts." Holmes interprets McCarthy's nondenial and acceptance as potential proof of his innocence, for if he were guilty he would have pretended to have had no involvement at all with his father. He also interprets McCarthy's discussion of his "desserts" as nothing more than the guilt of a grieving son who comes across his father's body. The duo then turns to James McCarthy's confession, which was given to the coroner who examined Charles McCarthy. According to the younger McCarthy, he had just arrived home from a three-day trip to Bristol when the murder occurred. His father had been out when he arrived back at the house, and had taken off for the lake after getting dropped off by a carriage in the yard of the house. While McCarthy headed in the direction of the lake, he heard him yell "Cooee!", a secret code word between father and son. After the younger McCarthy caught up with his father at the lake, he seemed surprised and irritated by his son's presence. This led to harsh words and nearly blows. "Seeming as [Charles McCarthy's] anger was becoming ungovernable," the younger McCarthy turned around and headed home. After 150 yards, however, he heard his father cry out, and ran back to the lake. There he found his father, dying from his head injuries; he dropped his gun and comforted his father, then ran to find the lodge-keeper.

The coroner then asked James McCarthy a series of questions. McCarthy explained the only thing his father said to him before he died was some bizarre mention of a rat; McCarthy had absolutely no idea what he meant. McCarthy refused to reveal why he had gotten into such a heated argument with his father at the lake, despite the coroner's multiple attempts to find out. Next, McCarthy explained he was completely puzzled why his father would utter the words "Cooee" given that James McCarthy did not know his son was in the area. Lastly, McCarthy said, though the frenzy of the moment fazed him, he did recall seeing some sort of grey-looking cloth about a dozen yards from his father as he lay down to cradle the dying man. When he stood up, however, the article had disappeared. He pointed out, however, that his back

was toward the article while he was holding his father.

Watson and Holmes arrive in the small country town of Ross, and meet Lestrade at the station. The three of them take a carriage to the Hereford Arms Hotel. Soon after their arrival, Alice Turner showed up to talk with them. Watson is taken aback by her youthful beauty. She is extremely relieved to see Sherlock Holmes, whose reputation is known far and wide. She says she is convinced James could not be the murderer because "he is too tender-hearted to hurt a fly." She adds she thinks she knows what James was arguing with his father about: the youngsters' relationship. Charles McCarthy, she says, has been insisting the two of them get married, but despite their long friendship, she and James are just friends. Also, she says, her father knew about Charles McCarthy's interest in the marriage, but he was very opposed to it. Holmes finds this information intriguing and asks to speak with Alice's father, but she says he is very sick and unable to receive any visitors. Charles McCarthy's death has struck him especially hard, because the two of them worked together in the gold mines of Victoria, Australia. She tells Holmes to send a message of support to James McCarthy when he visits him in jail, and then leaves the group. Lestrade upbraids Holmes for giving Alice false hope. Holmes responds he thinks he may be able to exonerate McCarthy, and he would like to see him. He and Lestrade take off for jail while Watson waits at the hotel.

While he waits anxiously at the hotel, Watson reviews an account of the murder in a recent local paper. He learns McCarthy's injuries were caused by a "heavy blow from a blunt weapon" and the victim must have been approached from behind, a potentially promising fact for James McCarthy's defense. He mulls over the rest of the oddities—the reference to the rat and the grey cloth—but can't make any sense of them. Later that night Sherlock Holmes returns alone to the hotel and fills Watson in on his conversation with the accused. He learned McCarthy was madly in love with Alice Turner, but he could not be with her because he had impulsively married a barmaid in Bristol while Turner was at boarding school for five years, a secret not known to either his father or Alice. He couldn't bring himself to tell his father this secret, however, because his father was "a very hard man." It explains his angry, frustrated response at the lake to his father, who was berating him for not proposing to Turner. After learning about McCarthy's charges, however, his wife in Bristol abandoned him, claiming she was already married to someone else. Holmes concludes McCarthy is innocent, and finding the perpetrator depends on resolving two clues: 1) who the elder

McCarthy had an appointment with at the lake; and 2) why he yelled "Cooee!" before he died.

The next day Watson, Lestrade, and Holmes return to Hatherley Farm and examine Charles McCarthy's and James McCarthy's boots. They make their way down to the lake where Charles McCarthy's body was found and to the nearby woods. The ground, which is so close to the lake, is still wet, and there are several footprint indentations in the earth. In the woods Holmes picks up a jagged stone. After his survey he concludes the murder was committed by "a tall man" who is "left-handed, limps with the right leg, wears thick-soled shooting boots and a grey cloak," and has other attributes. Lestrade is dubious and laughs at Holmes's conclusions.

Holmes discusses his findings with Watson back at the hotel. He says the McCarthy cried "Cooee"—an Australian greeting—because the person he was meeting was familiar with Australian slang. This fits with his finding that McCarthy's final mumblings about a "rat" was actually Ballarat, a city in Australia, in the Colony of Victoria. All that is left, he tells Watson, is to find "an Australian from Ballarat with a grey cloak." He explains to Watson he determined the man's height by the stride of the footprints at the crime scene, and that the man was left-handed.

Just as Holmes is about to reveal who the murderer is, John Turner limps into the hotel room. Holmes had sent him a note requesting the two speak at the hotel, lest Holmes's visit to Turner's house raise suspicions. Turner immediately confesses to the crime. He is distraught by the prospect of being arrested, but Holmes reassures him he is only a private investigator hired by his daughter. Relieved he explains what happened. Charles McCarthy, he says, was "a devil incarnate." The two met in Australia many years ago; as a young man Turner had gone to seek his fortune in the colony in the 1860s. He quickly fell in with the Ballarat Gang and started robbing supply wagons. One day he robbed McCarthy's wagon, leaving him alone but running off with the gold he was transporting. After this he returned to the Boscombe Valley, married, had Alice, and became a reformed man. One day, however, McCarthy showed up in town. He was able to blackmail Turner into giving him Hatherley Farm rent-free and other goods and services. One day, however, he demanded Alice—he wanted her to marry his son, James. This was too much for Turner; he'd rather die than give his precious daughter up to a McCarthy. And so he murdered Charles McCarthy. Holmes offers a way out to the sickly, distraught man: he would make a

full signed confession, which Holmes would keep to himself unless James McCarthy was sentenced to death. Turner gladly agreed to the scheme. He dies seven months later. James McCarthy is freed, once Holmes's findings cast sufficient doubt on his guilt, and he takes up with Alice Turner.

Analysis

"The Boscombe Valley Mystery" is set in a provincial area of rural England, but it's a global story that reflects the enormous power and reach of the British Empire in the late 19th century. The spark that set off the chain of events leading to the murder happened thousands of miles away in Australia, which at the time was a British colony. There are other indications of the British Empire's might. On the very first page we learn Watson was able to get his things together so quickly because of his military service in Afghanistan. Back in England the amenities of modern Britain are plain to see. The fact that Holmes and Watson travel to Boscombe Valley from London by train shows how well-connected the country is, and how expanded Holmes's reach is. Even Holmes, who has seen much and traveled all over, is taken with the country's new opportunities. After he explains to Watson how the case found him, he says, with no small amount of admiration, "and hence it is that two middle-aged gentlemen are flying westward at fifty miles an hour instead of quietly digesting their breakfasts at home."

On the train Holmes and Watson discuss the value of circumstantial evidence. Watson argues the circumstantial evidence points overwhelmingly toward James McCarthy's guilt, but Holmes, ever the patient teacher, counsels him to be more cautious. "It may seem to point very straight to one thing, but if you shift your own point of view a little, you may find it pointing in an equally uncompromising manner to something entirely different," he says. This nugget of wisdom, which stresses the importance of keeping an open, judgment-free mind, is typically Sherlockian.

This is the first story in the collection to involve Lestrade, the Scotland Yard detective. In so many ways he is Holmes's opposite and is meant to demonstrate the differences between the "official" authorities and the outsider Holmes. He is a pleasant fellow, but he is deeply conventional and unimaginative. In particular he is skeptical of Holmes's fancy logic work and hypothesizing. After Holmes wonders why Charles McCarthy felt so entitled to demand his son's marriage to Alice Turner, the daughter of McCarthy's seemingly generous benefactor, Lestrade dismisses his misgiving. "Do you not deduce something from that?" Holmes asks rhetorically. "We have got to the deductions and the inferences," Lestrade replies. "I find it hard enough to tackle facts, Holmes, without flying away after theories and fancies." He is a completely unoriginal investigator, and his incompetence is amplified by the fact that Holmes correctly solves the case even though both men are working on it.

The murder in this story reinforces Holmes's view—made more explicitly in later stories—that the countryside is far from an innocent, bucolic place. Behind the sparkling lakes, rustic cottages, and valley vistas, human nature lurks—often with tragic consequences. The isolation of the countryside evokes a feeling that horrors are simply out of sight. Indeed, a faint sense of foreboding increases the closer Holmes and Watson get to Boscombe Valley (and the farther they get from London, where crime is out in the open and plain to see).

The Five Orange Pips

Summary

On a particularly dark and stormy night in September 1887, a distraught young man from Horsham arrives at Holmes's Baker Street residence. His name is John Openshaw, and he is desperately seeking help in uncovering a sinister family mystery. The puzzle begins with his uncle, Elias Openshaw. Elias had gone to Florida before the American Civil War and amassed a small fortune as a planter. During the war he was a colonel in the Confederacy, but during Reconstruction he returned to the Horsham area because of his "aversion to the negroes." There he holed up in his house, alone, angry, and often drunk, accepting only his nephew John as a visitor. Despite his terrible disposition he doted somewhat on John, who by the age of 16 was all but running the household. John, however, was forbidden from entering a room in the attic, which Elias kept locked at all times.

In March 1883 Elias received a mysterious letter from an unknown sender. It was postmarked from Pondicherry (a city on the eastern coast of India), and contained no letter, only five dried orange pips (seeds). Scrawled on the inside flap were the

letters "K.K.K." The message sent Elias into tremors of shock. John asked him what was wrong, but he wouldn't explain anything, saying only "I'll checkmate them still." He then instructed John to send for a lawyer. When the lawyer and John convened in Elias's room, John noticed his uncle had burned a number of papers in his fireplace, and that a small brass box—which now stood empty—had the letter "K" inscribed on it in the same font as the letters on the postal letter he had received earlier in the day. In front of the lawyer Elias willed his estate to John's father, Joseph. Elias grew even more solitary and drunken over the next few weeks. Occasionally, however, he would erupt from his house, drunk, and skulk around his property. One night, however, he never returned home; he was soon found lying face-down in a pond by one of his gardens. No foul play was detected, and the death was ruled a suicide. Elias's house and holdings then passed on to John's father, Joseph Openshaw. Per Holmes's questioning, John confirms the letter was received on March 10, and Elias died on May 2.

John Openshaw's father Joseph moved into Elias Openshaw's house in early 1884. He examined the house for clues that might shed some light on his brother's death, but found only the empty brass box. Inside it had a label with the initials K.K.K. and "Letters, memoranda, receipts, and a register" written beneath. They also found some of his uncle's old papers, which revealed he had resisted Republican-led efforts to rebuild the South and enfranchise newly freed slaves. On January 4, 1885, Joseph Openshaw received a similar letter to the one his brother had received in 1883—an anonymous post with five dried orange pips inside and the letters K.K.K. written inside the envelope. Instructions were included on the envelope as well: "Put the papers on the sundial" in the house's garden. The message was postmarked from Dundee, a city in Scotland. Though he was deeply alarmed at first, Joseph resolved that this was merely a practical joke and refused John's pleas to go to the police. Three days later Joseph went to visit a friend in a nearby area. Two days after that, John received a telegram from the police informing him his father had fallen into a chalk pit and fractured his skull; by the time John arrived to visit him, his father was dead. As with his uncle, foul play was ruled out and Joseph Openshaw's death was ruled an accident.

John Openshaw inherited the estate, and lived unbothered for over two and a half years. Yesterday, he tells Holmes, he had received a letter with five orange pips; the message was postmarked from London—eastern division. It included the letters K.K.K. and another demand to "put the papers on the sundial." Desperate and afraid, Openshaw contacted the police, but they brushed him off, calling the affair a practical joke. "Incredible imbecility!" Holmes steams in response.

Holmes becomes extremely concerned for Openshaw's safety, and asks if he has any other clues that might help them figure out who is behind the letters. Openshaw produces a single paper he found on the floor of his uncle's room. The paper has the same bluish color of the papers his uncle burned, he tells Holmes. Written on the paper—in Elias Openshaw's handwriting—is a list of dates and short, cryptic phrases about interactions with different men, three of whom apparently received pips. Two of them "cleared," and the other was "visited." Holmes instructs Openshaw to immediately return home and put the paper and brass box out on his sundial, along with a note explaining all of Elias Openshaw's papers have been burned. He warns Openshaw to be careful and says he will find an answer to the riddle in London. Openshaw thanks him and leaves Holmes and Watson, and they begin discussing the situation. Holmes begins thinking aloud, and Watson both praises his thought process and ribs him a bit. They turn back to the case. Holmes realizes all of the letters were postmarked from seaports, which strongly suggests the letter-writer had been on a ship. He also observes that the lapse between the time the letters arrived and the time the deaths occurred means the letters were sent by "mail-boat" and the murderers came by sailing vessel. Thus there is a gap of seven weeks between the time Elias Openshaw received his letter and his death and a span of less than a week between the time Joseph Openshaw received his letter and his death. Since the newest letter came from London, then, it means John Openshaw is in immediate and grave danger. Holmes concludes the papers Elias Openshaw burned must have been extremely valuable, and that the deaths of the Openshaws were too professional for only one man to carry out.

Watson confesses his ignorance of the significance of the initials KKK, so Holmes instructs him to read the entry on the group in an American encyclopedia he has in his office. The entry explains the KKK, or Ku Klux Klan, was formed by ex-Confederate soldiers to terrify former slaves and whites who opposed the organization. It was a ruthlessly effective organization; anyone who opposed it was given an ultimatum to renounce their resistance, flee the country, or be killed. This seems to explain the puzzling entries on the blue paper John Openshaw found in his uncle's room. The encyclopedia entry explains the organization collapsed in 1869—the year Elias Openshaw returned to England.

The next morning Watson meets Holmes at the breakfast table. They look over the paper, and are horrified to learn John Openshaw died the previous night. According to the report he fell off the Waterloo Bridge as he was hurrying through the violent storm; the death was ruled an accident. For a few moments Holmes becomes silent. He resolves, however, to solve the mystery and heads out. He returns home that night and explains his findings to Watson. He spent the entire day looking over passenger ship records from 1883 onward. He discovered that a U.S. ship, *Lone Star*, had been to Pondicherry in January and February of 1883, Dundee in January 1885, and had been docked in London until this morning. Holmes learned there are only two Americans on the ship, which is currently bound for Savannah, Georgia. The culprits identified, Holmes sends a telegram to Savannah authorities informing them about the criminals onboard. Watson explains they never made it home, however, because the ship went down in the Atlantic.

Analysis

This story is as much of a thriller as it is a mystery. It begins as a typical whodunit. John Openshaw's visit seems to be about discovering the truth about his uncle's past. When we learn his uncle's death is suspicious, the story takes on a new layer of intrigue—doubly so when we learn his father's death is also suspicious. Eventually, however, it dawns on the characters (and the readers) John Openshaw *himself* is in grave danger. This gives the story a dramatic urgency that leaves the reader hanging on to every word of text. The reader hopes to see Openshaw escape from the clutches of the forces that killed his uncle and father, but isn't sure if he will. Doyle masterfully manipulates the reader into a state of emotional alarm. Holmes is not speaking just for himself when he urges John Openshaw to "above all, take care of yourself in the meanwhile, for I do not think that there can be a doubt that you are threatened by a very real and imminent danger."

Additionally, a sense of foreboding begins as soon as the story kicks off, and the descriptions of the severe weather only add to the unsettling atmosphere: "the equinoctial gales had set in with exceptional violence" in September 1883, Watson explains. It is under these circumstances that John Openshaw appears at Holmes's door, literally and figuratively traveling under black clouds. Also, Openshaw's isolation—he lives by himself, in the country—makes him seem especially vulnerable and again emphasizes Holmes's (Doyle's) belief that rural areas can be scary places. All alone in his country house, Openshaw is literally a waiting target.

John Openshaw, who is only in his early 20s, seems to be completely innocent, which compounds the reader's interest in his well-being. The death of his uncle, however, has a flat effect. He was an ex-Confederate colonel, opponent of Republican-led efforts to give freed slaves civil rights, and member of the Ku Klux Klan. In a way, then, his death at the hands of his former KKK associates could be interpreted as its own kind of justice given the brutal terror campaigns the group waged against black Americans and whites who opposed the organization. Because he was such a disreputable character, his death doesn't have much emotional impact. However, the death of Joseph Openshaw, who is innocent, and the grave danger John Upshaw finds himself in, inject the story with a heightened sense of drama, as typically occurs in tales that pit good against evil.

This story tells us a few things about Sherlock Holmes. One he has no other friends except for Dr. Watson. With Watson the generally serious and extremely composed investigator is able to (occasionally) let his guard down. As the two discuss the case after Openshaw has left, they take a rare break for small talk, during which Watson mildly pokes fun at Holmes's idiosyncrasies. The typically sober detective responds with a smirk, and pokes a bit of fun at himself. This demonstrates, yet again, the duo's intimate bond.

The Man with the Twisted Lip

Summary

Watson describes Isa Whitney, a man he knows who is addicted to opium. Whitney, Watson explains, followed the typical, sad trajectory of an addict: experimenting with the drug as a young man and eventually descending into physical and psychological ruin. One night in 1889 Whitney's wife arrives at the Watson household. She explains through tears that Isa had not been home for two days, and is most likely holed up in an opium den called Bar of Gold on Upper Swandam Lane, a notoriously slummy area of east London right by the River Thames. Watson agrees to search for Whitney at the den, promising to return with him if his friend is actually there. He takes a hired cab. As he approaches Upper Swandam Lane, he notes with alarm and a bit of scorn the neighborhood's

shabbiness. He enters the opium den and locates Whitney among the many other ne'er-do-wells. Whitney is dazed and confused, but he agrees to go home with Watson if he'll settle his tab.

As Watson looks for the den manager, a wrinkled old man whispers at him to "walk past me, and then look back at me." Watson does as he's told; when he looks back, he is astonished to see that the "old man" is Sherlock Holmes, slipped momentarily out of disguise. Holmes tells Watson to send Whitney home in the cab and to tell the cab driver to notify Watson's wife he's staying out with Holmes; he also directs Watson to meet him outside in five minutes. Watson meets Holmes outside as directed, and the two walk away from the den. Holmes, staying in character, limps for two streets. After confirming no one is following them, Holmes begins walking normally and explains himself to Watson. Holmes is looking for a man named Neville St. Clair, and his search brought him to the den. He is worried, however, because the den has a bad reputation for violence, and many men have disappeared through the trap door of the building, which leads directly to the wharf. "It is the vilest murder-trap on the whole riverside," he says. He then whistles out, and his cab materializes with a driver. He convinces Watson to accompany him to St. Clair's large villa near the town of Lee, seven miles outside the city, and sends his driver home.

As they drive out toward the house, Holmes explains the series of events that brought him to the Bar of Gold disguised as an elderly opium addict. The previous Monday the target of his search, Neville St. Clair, bid his wife farewell and went into London, as he does every morning. On Monday the happily married 37-year-old father of two went in earlier than usual, explaining to his wife he had two tasks to attend to. He also said he would pick up a gift of bricks for his son. That same day St. Clair's wife received a telegram informing her a package was waiting for her at a shipping office close to Upper Swandam Lane. After she retrieved the package she walked around the area; as she passed close to the Bar of Gold, she heard a cry coming from the building—and then looked up to see Mr. St. Clair staring at her and gesticulating as if he was in distress. He quickly disappeared back into the room, almost as if he'd been pulled into it. Before he disappeared, however, she noticed he was wearing his black coat but no collar or tie.

Mrs. St. Clair ran into the house, but the manager—a lascar (the term for a South or East Asian sailor)—prevented her from going upstairs. She ran outside and found a group of constables, who returned with her to the building and forced the manager to let them inspect the room Mrs. St. Clair had spotted her husband in. There was no trace of her husband, just a "crippled wretch" who swore he had never seen Neville St. Clair. Mrs. St. Clair spotted a box in the room. She opened it, revealing the set of bricks her husband had talked about that morning. This prompted the constables to inspect the room further. They found traces of blood on the windowsill and on the floor, and Neville St. Clair's clothes—with the exception of his coat—stashed behind the curtain. Apart from the blood there were no signs of foul play, leading to the conclusion that St. Clair must have left through the window, which overlooked a small strip between the building and the wharf. (At high tide it filled with water up to four and a half feet high.)

The lascar pleaded complete ignorance, and claimed to know nothing about the shabby man upstairs, a beggar well-known to the authorities named Hugh Boone. Holmes explains Boone is a professional beggar who rakes in a not-unimpressive amount of money from his daily perch in the city. Holmes attributes his success to Boone's unforgettable appearance—he has red hair and a disfiguring scar over his lip—and his quick wit. Boone protested his innocence and "declared that Mrs. St. Clair must have been either mad or dreaming" when she saw her husband at the window, but was arrested and taken to jail just the same. There were bloodstains on his shirt, but he said they came from his finger, which had a visible cut. When the inspectors went to check out the strip behind the building at low tide they found Neville St. Clair's coat, its pockets overstuffed with pennies and half-pennies. Holmes hypothesizes Boone is somehow involved in the disappearance but admits he is perplexed by the case.

The men arrive at the St. Clair villa and are greeted by Mrs. St. Clair, who has arranged for Holmes to stay on the premises while he works on the case. She asks Holmes to be frank with her and tell him if he thinks Neville St. Clair is dead; Holmes confesses he does think so. Mrs. St. Clair then produces a letter she received from Neville earlier that day. Holmes inspects the letter, which is postmarked from Gravesend, a town outside of London, and observes that the address seems to have been written in phases, suggesting the letter-writer wasn't initially sure of the address. He also notices the sloppy address handwriting is different than the handwriting of the letter itself. Mrs. St. Clair confirms the letter's handwriting, though hasty, matches her husband's. The letter is a quick note telling Mrs. St. Clair he is okay and the mystery will be revealed soon. Neville St. Clair's signet ring is included with the letter.

Further inspection reveals the letter was written on a blank page from a book, and the envelope must have been closed by someone with a "dirty thumb" who chewed tobacco.

Holmes goes over the facts of the story one more time with Mrs. St. Clair. She confirms everything Holmes has already been told but does agree it's possible her husband's "cry" was a shriek of surprise after seeing her, not a distress call. She also confirms her husband never used opium and had never said anything about the opium den. Holmes and Watson retire to their room. Watson turns in to sleep, but Holmes sets up the sofa cushions on the floor and sits, cross-legged, thinking and smoking his pipe atop the makeshift divan all night. At around 4:25 a.m. Watson awakes, and finds Holmes in the same position—though his huge pile of shag (tobacco) is gone. As they get ready to head out, Holmes tells Watson he thinks he has solved the case—and found the answer to the mystery in the bathroom. He doesn't disclose what he found in the bathroom, but he does say he has packed it into his bag. The two men take off for London and arrive at the jail, on Bow Street in central London, where Boone is being held. The men enter the jail building, and Holmes makes his way to the office of Inspector Bradstreet. After quick greetings Bradstreet leads him to Boone's cell.

Boone is sleeping when Holmes and Watson arrive outside his cell. The Inspector remarks on Boone's filthy state, and Holmes agrees Boone could benefit from a washing, adding he "took the liberty of bringing the tools with me." To Watson's amazement Holmes whips out a sponge from the bag he packed at the St. Clair household. Holmes asks Bradstreet to let him in Boone's cell so he may give him a wash; Bradstreet agrees, and opens the door. Holmes wets the sponge and wipes it twice across Boone's face. He then declares, "Let me introduce you ... to Mr. Neville St. Clair, of Lee, in the County of Kent." The prisoner's face skin is transformed from the washing from dirty and wrinkled to smooth. As he wakes up, Boone's "scar" falls away and his red hair falls off to reveal a head of dark hair. Shocked by the realization he has been found out, the prisoner buries his head in his pillow. He confesses he is indeed Mr. Neville St. Clair. He is terrified his children will find out about his ruse, and begs to know what he can do to keep the scandal from being reported in the news. Holmes says if the case goes to court there will be lots of publicity, but if St. Clair confesses right now to Bradstreet and explains why he shouldn't be charged, the case won't be known.

St. Clair thanks Holmes, and then tells his story from the beginning. He had guaranteed a loan for a friend, but when the friend went bust he was on the hook for paying the loan of £25. He had no idea where he would find the money, so in desperation he decided to go out begging for the funds—a role in which he had some experience. He acted in his youth, and his first adult job was newspaper reporter. While he worked at an evening paper he had went undercover to report on begging throughout London. He was so good at the disguise, however, he routinely made £2 in a day—as much as he made as a journalist in a week. When he realized how much money he could make begging he gave up his reporting job for begging full time. The money allowed him to grow fairly rich, marry, and purchase his large home. He used the room in the opium den where his wife spotted him as his base for changing in and out of his disguise. When he saw his wife he was dressing back into his regular clothes. He reacted in shock, which drew her to the building. He quickly changed back into his disguise, but only had time to get rid of his jacket, which he threw out the window, before his wife made her way into his room with the constables. The bloodstains were from his cut, which he reopened in his flurry to put on his disguise.

He slipped back into disguise because he was too ashamed to explain himself to his wife and family. To help alleviate his wife's worry, however, he sent her the letter—he scrawled in a rush—with his ring. He gave the letter to the lascar, who must have handed it off to some other visitor to the den, thus explaining its Gravesend postmark and odd address formatting. Bradstreet agreed to drop the case so long as St. Clair kills Hugh Boone for good; a grateful St. Clair readily agrees. The Inspector then asks Holmes how he cracked the case. "I reached this one ... by sitting upon five pillows and consuming an ounce of shag."

Analysis

In many ways this story evokes anxieties of city life, especially among the upper class. The area around the opium den, Upper Swandam Lane, is described in language usually reserved for horror stories. "Upper Swandam Lane is a vile alley lurking behind the high wharves which line the north side of the river to the east of London Bridge," observes Watson as he nears the den, which is "between a slop-shop and a gin-shop." As for the den itself, it had a feeling of "gloom"; the lights of opium pipes appeared through "black shadows." As for the people in the den, they were "bodies lying in strange fantastic poses." It's

perhaps not surprising the overseer of this sinful enterprise is a lascar—a foreigner. Victorian England was a global power, and as a result migration to England and contact with the world increased at this time. Suspicion of the foreign unknown followed. This den of depravity, which is managed by a foreigner, stands in stark contrast to the ordered and moral surroundings of Baker Street. It's a place that can grab even respectable men like Isa Whitney in its clutches.

The idea of upper-class shame resonates throughout the story. Whitney is pitied by Watson, and Neville St. Clair is so terrified of his family's discovering how he makes his living that he's willing to fake his own disappearance. The implication is that his faked disappearance scheme will somehow traumatize his family less than admitting to his begging career, a somewhat dubious calculation—at least to modern readers. The power of shame during Victorian England was perhaps strong enough that this calculation may have been a correct one.

In a bit of situational irony, it's the very power of Holmes's *own* pipe smoking that helps him crack this case, which is filled with despair about the horrors of opium addiction. Tobacco is different from opium, but it's still an addictive substance.

The Adventure of the Blue Carbuncle

Summary

Watson visits Baker Street a few days after Christmas. His visit is unannounced, but as always, Holmes is delighted to see him and implores his friend to stay and chat about his current investigation. When he enters he sees Holmes examining a worn felt hat. Watson half jokes the hat must be connected to some dastardly crime. Holmes laughs at his jest, explaining he's not sure whether it's related to a crime: he's merely interested in figuring out the history behind the hat. He then explains how he came into possession of the hat: it was brought to him on Christmas morning by a commissionaire named Peterson, who "[knows] that even the smallest problems are of interest to me." At four o'clock in the morning Peterson had been walking down Tottenham Court Road in London when he spotted the owner of the hat walking in front of him; he was a "tallish man," and was carrying a goose. When the man reached the corner a gang started menacing him and knocked off his hat. As the man tried to defend himself with his walking stick he accidentally smashed a shop window. Peterson ran toward him to help him, but the sight of Peterson and the smashed glass caused him to drop his goose and flee. The gang also took off at the sight of Peterson, leaving him with the goose and the hat.

Holmes says Peterson kept the goose until this morning, when he cooked it. He then turns to the hat and explains he has been busy trying to figure out information about its owner. The goose came with a note saying it was "For Mrs. Henry Baker," and the initials H.B. were marked inside the hat, but there are undoubtedly hundreds of Henry Bakers in London, so finding the owner requires further sleuthing. Watson is extremely skeptical that any valuable information could be revealed from merely looking at the article, but Holmes has deduced a large amount of information. He's certain of the following about the hat's owner: he is an intellectual; he was once affluent, but has fallen on hard times within the past three years; recently he has given in to some sort of vice, probably drinking; and his wife no longer loves him. When Watson interjects incredulously, Holmes adds the man is middle-aged, recently had a haircut, puts lime cream in his hair, and does not have gas service in his house.

To pacify Watson, who is still utterly unconvinced, Holmes explains what led him to these conclusions. Because the hat is large, it indicates the wearer had a large head (and thus a large brain and intellect). The hat is very expensive and high-quality, but its serious deterioration suggests its owner could not afford to replace it, presumably because he has faced economic hardship. His "foresight" is identifiable by the strap he added on to the hat. Holmes offers evidence for all of these claims, finishing with the assertion Henry Baker's wife didn't love him because the hat hasn't been brushed in weeks. Watson concedes to Holmes's superior deductions; as the men talk, however, Peterson bursts into the room. He holds out a shimmering blue stone, which he says his wife found in the bird's crop (a digestive area near the throat). Holmes identifies the stone as the Countess of Morcar's blue carbuncle; it was recently stolen out of the Countess's hotel room, and an ad offering a £1,000 reward has been running in local papers since the theft.

Holmes finds a newspaper account of the heist, which took place at the Hotel Cosmopolitan in London on December 22. A 26-year-old plumber named John Horner is accused of the crime and is now in jail. According to a hotel attendant named James Ryder, Horner had been summoned to the countess's dressing room to fix a grate. Ryder left the room for a bit, and when he returned Horner was gone and the (now-empty) box holding the stone was left on the dressing room table. The countess's maid, Catherine Cusack, heard Ryder's shouts, raced into the room, and ultimately confirmed his story. Horner was arrested by Inspector Bradstreet despite vigorously pleading innocence. The fact that he'd previously been convicted for robbery casts further doubt on his innocence.

Holmes tells Peterson and Watson they now have a responsibility to find the man whose hat they have and figure out his role in the carbuncle theft. He directs Peterson to place an advertisement in several evening newspapers; the ad should explain a hat and goose were found at the corner of Goodge Street and that Mr. Henry Baker can claim them both at Holmes's Baker Street residence at six thirty that same evening. Holmes and Watson discuss the stone's origins and characteristics, and then Watson leaves to make a doctor's call. He makes his way to Holmes's front door around six thirty, and spots a man—presumably Henry Baker—waiting outside. Once inside Holmes and Baker speak. Baker explains he didn't place an ad for his belongings because money is very tight. Baker is upset to hear Holmes has eaten the goose but is relieved when Holmes explains he obtained a new one for him. Holmes explains he still has all of the original bird's inner parts—including the crop—but Baker laughs and tells him he can keep them. Before Baker leaves, Holmes asks him where he purchased his goose. Baker says he acquired it from a pub called the Alpha Inn as part of a Christmas pool.

After dinner Holmes and Watson travel to the Alpha Inn. The proprietor tells them he acquired the set of geese—two dozen, to be exact—from a salesman named Breckinridge who works out of a stall at the Covent Garden Market. Watson and Holmes travel to the market, where they find Breckinridge. Holmes pretends to be interested in purchasing a goose, and asks Breckinridge where he sourced the geese he sold to the Alpha. Breckinridge explodes in anger, claiming people won't stop pestering him about the origins of the geese. He says he won't reveal his source. Playing along, Holmes bets him a five-sovereign coin the goose is "country bred." Breckinridge denies this, asserting his birds are "town bred"; Holmes demands proof, and Breckinridge shows him his ledger, which reveals Breckinridge purchased the birds from a woman named Mrs. Oakshott. Holmes makes a mental note of Oakshott's address, and leaves the angry salesman with his sovereign.

As Holmes and Watson debate whether or not to visit Mrs. Oakshott that evening, they hear a commotion coming from Breckinridge's stall. A "little rat-faced" fellow has been bothering the merchant, yet again, about his geese. An angry Breckinridge tells him to get lost; as the man slinks out Holmes corners him. Holmes introduces himself and explains he's been chasing information on a goose from Mrs. Oakshott to Henry Baker, and the man lights up with interest. Holmes hails a cab, and he, Watson, and the man talk. He claims his name is John Robinson, but after prodding from Holmes admits he is James Ryder, the attendant at the Hotel Cosmopolitan. The cab arrives at Holmes's house, and the men continue their discussion in Holmes's study. Holmes quickly gets Ryder to confess he was involved in the theft, though he blames it on Catherine Cusack, the countess's maid. Ryder pleads for mercy, but Holmes barks at him and tells him to think of the plumber Horner, who is in serious trouble. He demands Ryder to explain everything, which he does.

After Horner was arrested, Ryder knew he would be searched next, so he took off for his sister's. She is married to a Mr. Oakshott and raises fowls to be sold at the market. In his sister's yard he thought about what to do, and it dawned on him to seek the counsel of an ex-con friend. Eventually, he decided a trip to visit his friend would be too risky, so he considered other options. That's when he thought of the idea to hide the stone in a goose: his sister had promised him a bird for Christmas, so he picked one with a barred tail, then forced the stone down the goose's throat. When it came time for him to choose his goose, he insisted he wanted the bird with the barred tail; at first his sister resisted, but she eventually relented. He took the bird with the barred tail to his friend's place, but when they killed it, the stone was nowhere to be found. Ryder ran back to his sister's, but by this point all of the birds had been sold to Breckinridge. She explained there was another bird with a barred tail, and she could never tell the two geese apart, which explains why he has been harassing Breckinridge for information about his sales.

After hearing this Holmes kicks Ryder out of his house. Holmes turns to Watson and explains, as far as he is concerned, there is nothing more to be done. Ryder will never testify against Horner, which means the accused man will go free. As for Ryder, Holmes will not proceed with the case, as "it is the season for forgiveness."

Analysis

"The Adventure of the Blue Carbuncle" is noteworthy for how it organizes Holmes's sleuthing. In every Sherlock Holmes tale the masterfully astute detective makes no small number of deductions, but they usually involve multiple people or objects. In this story, however, all of Holmes's deductions come from a single object: Henry Baker's faded felt hat.

Additionally, none of Holmes's Baker-related deductions really contribute to the crime's solving. The hypotheses he makes about Baker during his discussion with Watson are proven correct once Baker comes to his house, but don't serve any greater purpose in the story. Actually getting Baker to his house merely required putting an advertisement in local papers, which Holmes could have done without any sort of deduction-making, given that he knew Baker's name from the note that came with the goose. Presumably, once Baker came to Holmes's house, Holmes could have figured out where he acquired the goose—from the Alpha Inn—even without knowing anything at all about Baker himself.

In fact in this story Holmes solves the crime merely by following the trail of the stone. This is good detective work, but it's not quite Sherlock Holmes-level detective work, which typically involves identifying clues no one else has seen and theorizing what they have to do with a crime. It's interesting, if not a touch disappointing, that Holmes's extreme deduction-making so early in the story doesn't really have a payoff. It seems to be largely for show.

As a result this story comes off more as a classic mystery and less a unique Sherlock Holmes tale. Even Holmes himself talks in a way that seems ripped from a jewel-thief caper. "Of course [the carbuncle] is a nucleus and focus of crime," he tells Watson, in a tone reminiscent of Sam Spade or Philip Marlowe. "Every good stone is. They are the devil's pet baits. In the larger and older jewels every facet may stand for a bloody deed."

The Adventure of the Speckled Band

Summary

Watson recalls an early adventure he had with Holmes around April 1883, involving a noble British family, the Roylotts of Stoke Moran; it was one of the first adventures Watson was involved in. Early in the morning a young woman pays a call to Baker Street in a deep state of distress. The woman, who is veiled and dressed in all black, introduces herself as Helen Stoner. She explains she lives with her stepfather in the decaying ancestral mansion of his family, the Roylotts, "one of the oldest Saxon families in England." Over the last four generations, however, the Roylotts have steadily descended into economic ruin.

Stoner and her twin sister Julia were born in India to a Major-General; their father died soon after their birth, however, and their mother married Dr. Grimesby Roylott, one of the Roylott family heirs, when the girls were only two. Roylott's father had been living in poverty in the family mansion, but Roylott had taken the initiative to move to Calcutta and start a medical practice. His practice was successful, but he had a terrible temper and in a fit of rage he beat one of his attendants to death. He served a long prison sentence and then returned to London bitter and angry. Shortly after the family arrived in England the Stoner girls' mother died, and Roylott took them to the Stoke Moran mansion. Their mother had bequeathed a sizable annual allowance to Roylott for taking care of the girls, with the condition that a portion of the allowance would be given to the girls after their marriage. In Stoke Moran Dr. Roylott became a social pariah because of his temper and willingness to fight. His only friends were groups of "wandering gypsies" he allowed to stay on his property, along with a baboon and a cheetah that were sent to him from India.

The girls' lives at the manor were dreary and lonely. Julia died two years ago, at the age of only 30. She died exactly two weeks after she was engaged to a "half-pay major of marines" whom she had met at the girls' aunt's house in a rare trip out. Helen has been haunted by her death, which is the reason why she has visited Holmes. She goes on to describe the circumstance surrounding Julia's death. First she explains that her, and her sister's, and Roylott's bedrooms are next to each other in the wing of the house that is still used (the rest of it has fallen into disrepair and is uninhabited). The night before she died, Julia—who slept in the middle room—went to Helen's room, unable to sleep because of the strong smell of Roylott's Indian cigars. Before she left she asked Helen if she had ever

heard a whistling sound in the middle of the night, but Helen said she hadn't, probably because she was a heavier sleeper. Julia left the room, and both sisters locked themselves into their rooms for the evening, a precaution against the animals roaming on the manor.

Helen says she couldn't sleep that night because she felt like something bad was going to happen. Her fears were realized when she heard Julia's blood-curdling scream in the middle of the night. As she ran down the corridor to Julia's room, she heard a vague whistling noise and the sound of clanging metal, but she couldn't identify either. Her sister convulsed in pain, and said these final words: "Oh my God! Helen! It was the band! The speckled band!" She pointed toward the doctor's room, and then lost consciousness. Roylott then rushed into the room, but despite his efforts and the efforts of a medical team that had been summoned, Julia died.

Holmes asks for clarification of a few points, which Helen gladly provides. She insists she heard whistling and a metallic sound, but she admits they might have just been sounds from an old house. She tells Holmes her sister was in her nightgown when she died and was found with a burned match in her hand; Holmes interprets this as an indication she saw something before she died. The coroner could find no cause of death—including poisoning, a typical cause in cases where there is no sign of violence—so Helen has chosen to believe she died of "pure fear and nervous shock" as a result of seeing something horrifying. She confirms there were gypsies around the manor at the time of Julia's death, and at Holmes's prodding speculates maybe the "band" Julia spoke of referred to a band of gypsies or the speckled handkerchiefs they wear.

Helen has lived a quiet life since her sister's death, but a month ago a longtime friend named Percy Armitage proposed to her and she accepted. (Her stepfather has given the marriage his blessing.) The previous night, however, she had a terrible scare. She was lying in bed in her sister's room—recent house repairs put Helen's room out of commission—when she heard a whistling noise. She jumped up, terrified, and immediately lit the lamp in her room, but she didn't see anything. She was too scared to sleep, however, so she stayed up all night and traveled to see Holmes first thing in the morning. Holmes asks her if she has told him everything; she claims she has, but when Holmes points out bruises on her wrist she admits her stepfather has been rough with her.

Holmes says that too much is unknown and that he must visit

Stoke Moran that day to investigate. Helen agrees to meet Holmes and Watson at the house that afternoon and then leaves. Holmes and Watson mull over the perplexing case. Holmes offers this working hypothesis: Roylott enlisted the help of the "band" of gypsies to break into Julia's room from the outside of the house (thus the "metallic" sound of shutters being pried opened and closed). Watson is skeptical, and Holmes agrees he really doesn't know what to think. While they are talking a huge man stalks into the room. He identifies himself as Grimesby Roylott, and demands to know what his stepdaughter has told the men. Holmes plays coy, and Roylott leaves in a huff, but not before warning the men to stay away from Helen. An unflustered Holmes laughs off the showdown and tells Watson he must leave for some time. He returns to Baker Street at one o'clock after having spent time researching the Roylott family's finances. He found that the family's income is now only £750, and because of the will stipulation each daughter is guaranteed a payment of £250 upon marriage. This convinces him Roylott had a strong motive for killing Julia, and that he and Watson must get to Stoke Moran immediately to protect Helen. Holmes instructs Watson to get his pistol ready, and the two head out toward the mansion. They take a train from London and then pick up a cab for the last five miles to the house.

They walk up to the house and meet Helen Stoner. Holmes tells her about their meeting with her stepfather, which unsettles her. She leads the men to the front of the wing that is in use, just outside the bedroom windows. There are some superficial signs of construction outside the last room (Helen's old room), but she says there were no issues with her room and surmises the "repairs" were a ploy to move her into her sister's old room. Holmes inspects the metal shutters on Julia's room, and concludes they can't be breached when they are closed.

Next they enter the mansion and examine Julia's old room. Holmes observes a ventilator (air vent) in the ceiling that opens into Roylott's room, which is adjacent. There's also a bell hanging from the ceiling with a long, thick pull that extends all the way to the bed's pillow, but after further inspection he determines the bell is a dummy: it hangs from a hook right next to the ventilator, and thus it cannot communicate with any other room in the house. When Holmes asks Helen about the bell, she says it was installed a few years ago, around the same time the ventilator was fitted, though her sister hadn't actually requested either. The group then moves on to Roylott's room. The doctor's room is similarly spare and basic as Julia's, but it

contains a safe and a wooden chair that backs up against the wall Roylott shares with Julia. He also spots a saucer of milk and a dog leash that has been curled up and manipulated into a whipcord.

Holmes is satisfied but alarmed by his findings, and he instructs Helen to follow his instructions exactly lest the fate of her sister befall her, too: he and Watson will hole up in a nearby inn through sundown. When her stepfather goes to his room for bed, Helen is to light up her room with her lamp, which will signal Holmes and Watson (who will have a clear view of the mansion from the inn) to come to the house, entering through the window in Julia's old room. At that point Helen is to move into her old room—the one currently undergoing repair—and Holmes and Watson will move into Julia's room. Helen agrees to this plan, and Holmes and Watson take off for their temporary lodgings.

Settled in a room at the Crown Inn, the pair watches as Roylott's hulking figure makes his way across the property and returns to the mansion at dusk. As they wait for Helen's signal, Holmes expands on his findings in Julia's and Roylott's rooms. He says he knew a ventilator was installed between the rooms before he even viewed them because of Julia's complaints about Roylott's cigars. He noticed the bed in her room is bolted to the floor, next to the bell and the ventilator. The fact that the ventilator and dummy bell were installed right before her death means they had some role in her death. As for what role, the two of them will find out themselves that evening. At eleven o'clock a light appears in Helen's room, and the two men set out for the mansion. Once they're on the lawn, they see what appears to be a "hideous and distorted child" running across the grass. Horror turns to laughter when they realize it is the resident baboon. The two men noiselessly make their way into the room, close the shutters, and wait—Watson armed with a pistol and Holmes with a cane.

Just past 3:00 a.m., a momentary flash of light appears through the ventilator. The smell of a lantern being lit follows. Thirty minutes later, they hear a new noise: "a very gentle, soothing sound, like that of a jet of escaping continually from a kettle." At the first trace of this strange noise Holmes lights a match and then starts beating the bell pull with his cane; Watson cannot see anything except for Holmes's terror-stricken face. A few moments later, however, a tortured scream comes from Roylott's bedroom. Watson and Holmes enter his bedroom, Watson with his gun cocked. In the room Roylott is lying dead in his bedclothes; there's a "peculiar yellow band, with brownish speckles," wrapped around his forehead. Watson takes a step and sees the band is actually a swamp adder, "the deadliest snake in India," according to Holmes. Holmes wraps the dog leash around the snake and leads it into the safe.

The next day Holmes and Watson send Helen to her aunt's house. On their way to Baker Street, Holmes debriefs Watson on how he uncovered the plot. At first he thought Julia Stoner's dying remarks about a "band" referred to the gypsies roaming the premises, but after he surveyed her old room and Doctor Roylott's old room he realized Julia's killer must have come from inside the house. Roylott's interest in dangerous animals from India strengthened his conviction. A poisonous snake would be the perfect murder weapon, because it would kill without leaving a trace of the kind of poison any coroner would check for. Holmes confirmed his hunch after examining the wooden chair in Roylott's room; its marks indicated the chair had been stood upon, no doubt so Roylott could reach the ventilator. The milk, dog leash, and safe—which makes a clanging sound when closed—further confirmed Holmes's suspicions. Despite the fact that he saved Helen Stoner's life and solved her sister's murder, he says the death of Roylott "is likely to weigh very heavily upon my conscience."

Analysis

"The Adventure of the Speckled Band" has all of the elements of a classic Sherlock Holmes mystery, but it's also an example of a gothic horror tale. The setting—a decrepit country mansion inhabited by the brutish and troubled heir of a once-powerful dynasty—evokes a deep sense of dread, and it could just as easily be included in any work by Edgar Allan Poe, Mary Shelley, or Bram Stoker (whose name, it's worth mentioning, bears a close resemblance to Stoke Moran). The exotic and dangerous animals and groups of gypsies that roam freely across the manor add another layer of danger to the Roylott homestead, which would be quite spooky even without them. The cumulative effect is of a sinister, haunted place.

This volatile setting challenges, yet again, romantic views of rural areas. There are no laughing cows and friendly farmers at Stoke Moran—but there is a rampaging baboon. Far from idyllic, rural isolation is depicted as creepy and dangerous. The more the reader learns about the manor, the more the reader fears for Helen Stoner, who is left to fend for herself in the midst of such madness. As a result Holmes's unfolding

investigation takes on a dramatic sense of urgency, and readers cannot but turn the pages, wondering: will Holmes save Helen Stoner or not? "Twelve struck, and one and two and three, and still we sat waiting silently for whatever might befall," Watson says gravely, as he and Holmes linger in literal and figurative darkness in Julie Stoner's lethal bedroom. This is a thriller disguised as a deduction-based mystery.

Roylott himself is a perfectly scary figure: hulking, menacing, and troubled by a violent past. Violence seems to lurk whenever he's around. Watson's descriptions of Roylott as he arrives home by cab paint a monster in human form. From their perch at the Crown Inn Watson and Holmes observe Roylott's "huge form looming up beside the little figure of the lad who drove him"; they hear "the hoarse roar of the doctor's voice" and see "the fury with which he shook his clenched fists at [the boy]."

Additional details give the story an air of creepiness. There's the "hideous and distorted child" that turns out to be the roaming baboon imported from the Orient. The house itself, an epitome of faded grandeur, is designed in a bizarre style with wings "like the claws of a crab." Even Helen Stoner, the damsel in distress, seems to be a bit off. Her face is "drawn and grey," and her hair is "shot with premature" grey; she has eyes "like those of some hunted animal," Watson observes. When she visits Baker Street, she's dressed in black from head to toe and is even wearing a veil, an article of clothing usually associated with funerals and death.

Despite the sinister feeling throughout the story, there are moments of levity throughout it. Roylott's visit to Baker Street is especially absurd. When his over-the-top descriptions of his adversary—"Holmes, the meddler"; "Holmes, the busybody"; and "Holmes, the Scotland Yard Jack-in-Office"—are juxtaposed with Holmes's nonchalant responses, the effect is comical. "He seems a very amiable person," Holmes deadpans to Watson moments after his fire poker is so rudely assaulted. Right after this Holmes pretends to be angry over the fact that Roylott thinks he is from Scotland Yard. "Fancy his having the insolence to confound me with the official detective force!" he fake-complains to Watson. This scene temporarily lightens the mood of an otherwise deeply spooky tale.

The Adventure of the Engineer's Thumb

Summary

Watson confesses this is only one of two adventures initiated by him and not Holmes. Early one morning in 1889, Watson is awoken at his house (which doubles as his practice) by a man in need of medical care. He has come from Paddington Station, London's main rail depot. The man introduces himself as Victor Hatherley, and he is in a poor state. One of his hands is wrapped in a bloody handkerchief, and he seems to be on the cusp of a nervous breakdown. He removes the handkerchief to reveal a gory mess where his thumb once was. As Watson dresses Hatherley's wound he gradually regains his composure, and he explains to Watson that the previous night he was the victim of a "very murderous" attack. Hatherley says he is planning to talk to the police, but he is worried they won't believe his "very extraordinary" story. Watson suggests that Hatherley pay a visit to Holmes, and he readily agrees, saying he has heard of the famous detective.

When Watson and Hatherley arrive at Holmes's house the detective is smoking a "before-breakfast pipe" and reading the paper. He invites his visitors to have breakfast with him, and asks Hatherley to tell his story. Hatherley begins by discussing his background. He is a hydraulic engineer, and two years ago he left a company he had been working for to start his own firm. His new business has struggled severely, however. It was a (very) pleasant surprise, therefore, when a man came into his office the previous day praising Hatherley's reputation and offering him a job for 50 guineas. The man was a singular character, to use a favorite description of Holmes. He was extremely thin, looked to be around 40 years old, and had a trace of German accent. His business card said his name was Colonel Lysander Stark, and he repeatedly demanded Hatherley's work remain absolutely secret.

Colonel Stark asked if Hatherley could visit his property, seven miles from the Eyford train station, in the country, that evening. Hatherley, whose office is in London, protested at first because this would keep him out past the last train back to London. Colonel Stark, however, promised to pay him for the inconvenience. With Hatherley's agreement in hand, Stark explained the situation. He said he recently discovered

deposits of fuller's earth, a type of clay that has cosmetic and industrial uses, on his property. The majority of the deposits, however, ran underneath the land of his neighbors to his left and right. He intended to purchase the adjacent properties before their owners realized the (high) value of the lands, but he didn't have enough money to buy them out. To raise money he has been drilling on his own plot, in secret, with the help from some of his friends.

Hatherley said he understood the predicament, but he wondered why Stark was using a hydraulic press to excavate fuller's earth, since the material is typically "dug out like gravel from a pit." Stark dismissed him, explaining "we have our own process." He then thanked Hatherley for his discretion and asked him to confirm he would be at the Eyford station at 11:15 that evening, which he did. After Stark departed, Hatherley thought long and hard about taking the job, but despite his deep misgivings he traveled to Eyford on the last train. When he arrived he saw the only other person at the station was a dozing porter. Stark greeted him and was ushered into a cab pulled by a single fresh horse; he immediately covered the windows inside the cab. They traveled at a rapid pace over worn country roads for over an hour, despite the fact that Stark claimed to live only seven miles from the station. When the cab eventually pulled up to a house, Stark pushed Hatherley inside and shut the door so quickly he was unable to get any sense of the place.

Hatherley then spotted a woman approaching from down the hall. She was pretty, well-dressed, and spoke a few words in a foreign language to Stark, who sent her away. He asked Hatherley to wait for a few moments in a small room and then left. Hatherley surveyed the room and saw books on science and poetry in German. The door abruptly opened, and the woman was standing at the entrance. She appeared distraught, and she warned Hatherley, quietly and in broken English, he should leave immediately. Hatherley considered her advice but figured he had come this far, and the fee was so good, that he'd stick the project out. There was a sound of footsteps upstairs, and the woman left the room. Stark entered along with a fat man named Mr. Ferguson, who, according to Stark, was his secretary and manager. Stark said it's time to see the press. Hatherley was surprised to learn the machine was actually inside the house, but Stark deflected the question, saying it's because they compress the fuller's earth inside.

Stark led Hatherley upstairs and through the large, labyrinthine house, which was clearly falling apart. The site of peeling plaster and mold unnerved Hatherley, but he kept a straight face. The men stopped in front of a small door. Stark directed Hatherley through the door into a tiny chamber; they were inside the press, standing underneath the descending piston. Stark explained the piston seems to have been losing force for some reason, and asked Hatherley to diagnose the problem. Hatherley examined the machinery and discovered a problem with the driving rod, which he conveyed to Stark and Ferguson. He also concluded the machine was clearly not being used to process fuller's earth. He saw a metallic crust accumulated on the floor of the piston chamber, and as he moved to inspect it further Stark asked what he was doing. Hatherley replied, a bit rashly, that if he knew the true purpose of the machine he would have been better equipped to troubleshoot it. This seemed to enrage the colonel, who replied, "You shall know all about the machine." He then stepped out of the room, locked the door, and started the hydraulic press's engine. As the roof of the room—in actuality, the descending piston—descended on him, he searched frantically for an escape. At the last moment he spied a ray of light coming through one of the walls and threw himself through it, landing in a corridor; moments later he heard the crunch of the lantern he had been using underneath the piston.

As he picked himself up he saw the woman again, and she frantically directed him into a bedroom with a window. Hatherley hung from the windowsill, which sat about 30 feet above a garden. Stark barged into the room cursing the woman, Elise; he had a meat cleaver in one of his hands. She begged "Fritz" to leave Hatherley alone, imploring him to "remember your promise after the last time." Fritz (Stark) waved her off, claiming Hatherley "has seen too much." He then charged toward the windowsill and swiped the cleaver at Hatherley, who fell into the garden. Hatherley ran away, but as he was escaping he looked down at his hand and saw the bloody place where his thumb used to be. He was able to tie his handkerchief around his hand before he fainted in an area of rosebushes.

He awoke in a hedge as the sun was coming up. He stood up to get his bearings and was shocked to see he was within walking distance of Eyford Station; neither the Germans' house, nor their garden, was within view. He walked to the train station and found the sleepy porter whom he spotted the night before, but the porter said he didn't know anything about a man named Colonel Lysander Stark nor the carriage that picked Hatherley up. He took the first train back to London and then made his way to Watson's practice.

Holmes sits contemplatively, and then pulls a year-old missing persons notice from his large archive. It asks for information about a 26-year-old hydraulic engineer who left home at ten o'clock at night and hasn't been seen since. Hatherley gasps at the connection, which confirms the woman's remarks about "the last time." Per Holmes's suggestion, the three men go to Scotland Yard, where they tell the story to Inspector Bradstreet. The group—which now includes Bradstreet and a plainclothes officer—set off for Eyford Station by train.

During the ride they brainstorm where the Germans' house might be located. Hatherley is at a loss, but he contends someone from the group must have picked him up and dropped him off near the station. Given the large distance his carriage traveled to the house—about 12 miles, by his estimate—there's no way he could have walked far in his bleeding daze. Bradstreet pulls out a map of the area, and each man—except for Holmes—hypothesizes where the house might be located. Holmes points to the center of the map—the village of Eyford—and asserts this is where the house is. He says the horse carriage must have traveled six miles out of town and then six miles back; there's no way the horse could have been fresh (per Hatherley's description) if it had just traveled over rough roads from a house 12 miles away. Bradstreet agrees with Holmes's reasoning, and then says Hatherley has very likely stumbled upon a well-known gang of coin counterfeiters.

As the train pulls into Eyford Station the group sees a cloud of smoke rising from a house nearby. The stationmaster says the house is owned by an Englishman named Dr. Becher, but a slim foreign man has been staying with him. The group takes off for the house; when they arrive Hatherley confirms it's the very structure he was on the previous night. Neither Colonel Stark, Ferguson, or the German woman can be found. Holmes concludes Hatherley's lamp, which was crushed by the piston, must have accidentally started the fire.

Earlier that morning a villager had come across a group ferrying large boxes toward the town of Reading, but that was the last time the culprits were seen. Watson also explains that stocks of nickel and tin were discovered on the premises, but no coins. He speculates the bounty must have been transported in the boxes. The firefighters, however, did come across Hatherley's thumb. Also, a series of large and small footprints tracking from the rosebushes where Hatherley passed out to the hedges where he woke up revealed he must have been carried to safety by the woman and Ferguson. The men take the train back to London.

Analysis

This adventure, like most, begins with a bit of preamble from Watson. He points out this investigation is unique not only because he, not Holmes, initiated it, but also because it was "so dramatic in its details." This is certainly true; after all, it's not every day we meet skinny German coin counterfeiters working under the alias Colonel Lysander Stark. In addition the idea of a man-chomping hydraulic press hidden inside a house is as bizarre as it is bold. This introduction leads to a smart reflection from Watson: stories are much less interesting when they are reported matter-of-factly in the press. Rather, they have their greatest power "when the facts slowly evolve before your own eyes, and the mystery clears gradually away as each new discovery furnishes a step which leads on to the complete truth." This is an excellent expression of the ethos of Watson and Holmes—and of Doyle himself, who has so expertly created these exact kinds of stories.

This story seems to have a hidden message buried beneath its entertaining plot: trust your gut. Numerous times alarm bells go off in Hatherley's mind throughout the story warning him to bail on this job. He's not greedy, but he is desperate for work, so the prospect of making 50 guineas—ten times his normal fee for the kind of service he was providing—blinds him to the multiple red flags in his way. Looking back on his adventure, Hatherley realizes as much. He explains to Watson and Holmes that he had serious doubts about the job as soon as Colonel Stark left his office: "The face and manner of my patron had made an unpleasant impression upon me, and I could not think that his explanation for the fuller's earth was sufficient to explain the necessity for my coming at midnight." And yet, he pressed on. Even when he was explicitly warned to leave and was told something bad was afoot by the German woman, he still pressed on. One could argue Hatherley's deception of himself is almost as intense as the plot perpetrated by the gang of counterfeiters. At the very end of the story, on the train back to London, he laments his plight to his co-investigators. "I have lost my thumb and I have lost a fifty-guinea fee, and what have I gained?" he asks. "Experience," Holmes replies, driving home the message of the story.

As is the case in so many other stories in this collection, the countryside is the setting of the crime in this one. The counterfeiters exploited the isolation offered by their rural environment to run their operation and to attack Hatherley (and his predecessor, who was presumably killed "the last time"). Far away from prying eyes, all sorts of bad things can be done with impunity.

Lastly, the title of this story, "The Adventure of the Engineer's Thumb," is a bit cheeky. Most of the story titles in this collection are straightforward: they simply name the main person, thing, or event at the center of the tale. While it's true the engineer's thumb had an "adventure," if you can call it that, it's only part of the larger story. It's clear Doyle was putting a clever, morbid spin on the titling conventions.

The Adventure of the Noble Bachelor

Summary

A few weeks before Watson's wedding when he is living at Baker Street with Holmes, Holmes returns home one afternoon to find a letter in a fancy envelope waiting for him. To his surprise (and delight) it's not an invitation to a social function, but a request from a nobleman, Lord St. Simon. The letter explains St. Simon would like to speak with Holmes about the "very painful event" that occurred at his wedding. He says he has already discussed the situation with Lestrade, the Scotland Yard detective, but he would like to review the case with Holmes as well. As a result he will be visiting Baker Street at 4:00 p.m. that day. It's already 3:00 p.m. when Holmes gets the letter, so he spends the next hour reviewing St. Simon's case. With Watson's help he digs through his archives. He learns Lord Robert Walsingham de Vere St. Simon is 41 and comes from a long line of famed British nobility.

Watson then directs his attention to recent newspaper mentions of St. Simon. The first paper, published a few weeks earlier, contains a section announcing the wedding between St. Simon and a San Francisco woman named Hatty Doran. Her father is Aloysius Doran, a lawyer, and she is his only daughter. The next story they review is from a society paper published the same week. This paper explains Aloysius Doran is a millionaire, and St. Simon will likely net a six-figure dowry from marrying the beautiful young heiress. This will come in handy, as his family fortune is severely diminished and the only property he has left is a small estate called Birchmoor. Other papers provide further details about the wedding: it will take place at St. George's church; only half a dozen friends are invited to the ceremony; the reception will take place at the large house Aloysius Doran has rented in London; and the honeymoon will be taken at Lord Backwater's estate.

Given all of this information, Watson is shocked when Holmes explains Hatty Doran disappeared at the reception. The men turn their attention to the most recent paper, published the day before, which gives an account of the disappearance. According to the report the morning ceremony proceeded without incident, and the small wedding party made its way to Aloysius Doran's rented house. During breakfast, however, an unidentified woman forced her way into the house "alleging that she had some claim upon Lord St Simon"; she was forcibly ejected from the premises but not before causing a huge scene. While the bride ate breakfast with the wedding party she excused herself and went up to her room. When she didn't return her father went looking for her, but the servants in the house told him she went to her room only to grab her coat and hat and then fled the house. Aloysius Doran contacted the police, and they arrested the woman who caused the incident at the reception, a former dancer named Flora Millar who has known St. Simon "for some years."

The doorbell rings at Baker Street, and St. Simon enters. Watson observes their visitor is predictably patrician looking, but he comes off older than his age, and he dresses "to the verge of foppishness." Holmes and St. Simon make small talk, and then Holmes gets down to questioning. St. Simon says he and Hatty Doran met—but did not become engaged—in San Francisco the previous year, while St. Simon was on vacation in America. Her father, "the richest man on the Pacific slope," made his fortune in gold mining and investing—but she was 20 years old when the family became rich. Before she was catapulted to the upper crust she was a tomboy who explored the outdoors and knew her way around mining camps. He adds she has a "volcanic" temper and is tremendously strong-willed. Hatty and her father came to London during the previous season, and after a few meetings the couple became engaged.

St. Simon asserts nothing was out of the ordinary during their wedding day, but he recalls a minor incident. As Hatty Doran was walking down the aisle she dropped her bouquet into a pew, and a man handed it back to her. It didn't seem like a big deal, but when St. Simon discussed the incident with her in their cab to the reception she made a huge fuss about it. Per

Holmes's questioning, St. Simon confirms the man wasn't a member of the wedding party, just a member of the public visiting the church that morning. When the couple arrived back to the house, Hatty went directly to speak with her maid, Alice, whom she had brought from California and was particularly close with. St. Simon didn't pay much attention to the conversation, but he heard his wife utter the saying "jumping a claim," which he didn't understand because it was American slang. After this exchange she sat down for breakfast. Ten minutes later she "muttered some words of apology" and then fled the house. She was spotted later walking in Hyde Park with Flora Millar.

Holmes asks St. Simon about his relationship with Millar. He says he has been on "a very friendly footing" with the dancer, but he has always been kind to her. Still, she has a terrible temper and is extremely possessive of St. Simon, which is why he planned such a low-key wedding. He had expected her to show up at Aloysius Doran's house during the reception, so he hired plainclothes police officers to guard the premises; they threw Millar out after she showed up and caused a racket. Hatty Doran didn't witness Millar's disruption, yet she was later spotted with Millar. The police think Millar may have somehow tricked Doran into leaving, St. Simon says, but that's about as far as their theorizing goes. St. Simon's theory is his wife decided entering British high society was too intense and too different from her carefree days in America, so she ran off.

Holmes asks St. Simon one clarifying question: where was his position at the breakfast table? He responds that he could see the street and the park through the window. Holmes tells St. Simon he believes he has solved the case and will get back to him shortly once he confirms Hatty's whereabouts. St. Simon leaves Baker Street and shortly after Lestrade enters. A frustrated Lestrade says he has directed police to search for Doran's body in the Serpentine, a lake inside Hyde Park. When Holmes doubts this approach, Lestrade angrily produces a waterlogged bridal dress and other wedding-day accouterments. There's a note inside the dress: "You will see me when all is ready. Come at once." It's signed with the initials "F.H.M.," which obviously implicates Flora Millar in Doran's disappearance, Lestrade argues. Holmes turns the note over and sees a list of hotel charges. He argues this bill fragment is the most important information for the case, but Lestrade denounces Holmes's armchair reasoning and leaves Baker Street in a huff. Before he exits, however, Holmes offers his rival a clue: "Lady St. Simon is a myth."

Holmes leaves Baker Street to investigate the matter further, leaving Watson at home. An hour later, around 5:00 p.m., a large delivery of food arrives without explanation. At around 9:00 Holmes returns to Baker Street. He is glad to see dinner has arrived, and says that company should be arriving any minute. St. Simon arrives looking upset. He confirms a message Holmes sent had reached him, and it unsettled him greatly. He alludes to some sort of embarrassment, but Holmes assures him whatever happened "is the purest accident." The door rings, and a couple enter the house; Holmes introduces them to St. Simon as Mr. and Mrs. Francis Hay Moulton.

The sight of his wife—nay, Mrs. Moulton, formerly Hatty Doran—repels St. Simon, but she tries to sympathize with his distress. St. Simon continues to respond bitterly, but upon Holmes's urging she offers her side of the story. She explains she and Frank (the man she's with) met in a mining camp in the Rockies in 1884 and became engaged. Hatty's father struck gold in the camp and became very wealthy, but Frank had no similar luck. As a result Hatty's father called off the engagement and moved the family to San Francisco. Frank followed them to San Francisco, secretly, and the couple vowed to be together as soon as Frank made his fortune. Before he left, however, the couple married in secret. Hatty followed Frank's movements around the country. One day a newspaper reported he had been killed during an Apache raid, and Hatty had a breakdown. A year later she met St. Simon in California. She decided to remarry when her father moved the family to London, partly to please her father, but she still longed for Frank. However, she says, she intended to be a good wife to St. Simon and to throw herself into the marriage.

On her wedding day, as she made her way down the aisle, she spotted Frank in the front pew. Though dazed, she decided to go through with the wedding rather than cause a scene. She saw him writing a note. On her way out she purposely dropped her bouquet in front of Frank, who handed it back to her along with his note. When she got back to the house she told her maid (who was a close confidant) everything. While she was thinking about what to do over breakfast, she saw Frank through the window. He beckoned for her to come follow him toward the park. That's when she ran up to her room and then slipped out of the house. As she was in the park "some woman"—Flora Millar, no doubt—came up to her alleging St. Simon had skeletons in his closet, but she shook her off and found Frank. He explained he had been taken prisoner by the Apaches but escaped to San Francisco. While he was there he read about Hatty's upcoming wedding, so he traveled all the

way to London to find her.

Hatty says despite her happiness at finding Frank she was ashamed of leaving St. Simon the way she did. She thought it would be best for everyone if she completely vanished, so Frank put her clothes together and hid them in Hyde Park. When Holmes visited her earlier this evening and made the case that she owed St. Simon an explanation, however, she reconsidered her plan and agreed to come to Holmes's house. She asks St. Simon, her (brief) second husband, for his forgiveness. St. Simon shakes her hand, but insists he doesn't like to air personal business in front of any group, and leaves the house after turning down Holmes's invitation to dine together. The remaining foursome eats dinner.

After the Moultons leave, Holmes explains to Watson how he cracked the case. Hatty Doran's strange behavior on her wedding day must have been triggered by something from her past, he says. Because she had spent so little time in London, this trigger must have come from America. When St. Simon described the man in the first pew, Hatty's bouquet dropping—an obvious ruse—and her talk with her maid about "jumping a claim," Holmes knew she had run off to be with another man. He tracked her down through the hotel receipt found with her clothes. The prices on the bill indicated that whoever wrote the note had been staying at a very expensive place, so Holmes narrowed his search to the most expensive hotels in the city. The ledger of the second hotel he visited indicated that an American named Francis H. Moulton—initials F.H.M.—had recently stayed there. After inquiring about the man, Holmes was given a London address where the man's mail was to be forwarded, and that's where he found the couple.

Analysis

The plot of "The Adventure of the Noble Bachelor" is a bit lighter than many of Holmes's other investigations. No one is killed or placed at risk of being killed, nor does anyone's thumb go on a separate adventure from his body, and no actual crime is committed (except, perhaps for a crime of the heart). It's a fairly conventional mystery that takes the reader along as the characters confront—and discard—one potential theory after the next. With Holmes as the guide through the zigs and zags, this domestic drama becomes much more interesting than if it were simply a story of a runaway bride.

This story also reveals much about social class in the late 19th century, particularly the upper class. The gossipy society papers—one of which Holmes relies on for information about the St. Simons' marriage—reveal the values and insecurities of the age. Snobbishly but cleverly, the paper Holmes consults spells out the mutual benefits of the wedding transaction between Lord St. Simon and Hatty Doran: the economically humbled Lord will gain access to her family's fabulous California riches, and she will "transition from a Republican lady to a British peeress." It's intriguing St. Simon is willing to go along with such a nakedly opportunistic coupling despite his obvious upper-class pretensions. The first time he arrives at Baker Street, Watson finds him almost a caricature of an English aristocrat; St. Simon, he observed, had the "well-opened eye of a man whose pleasant lot it had ever been to command and to be obeyed."

Perhaps he's willing to make an exception because his bride-to-be (and fortune-to-be) is American. Among the British upper class, nothing was less distasteful than new money. And yet, Aloysius Doran is an entirely self-made man, a complete contrast to the "foppish," entitled St. Simon, a "gentleman" whose financial status is tenuous but whose social status remains as high as ever. In the end, however, Hatty opts for love, not status, a twist that suggests Doyle was sympathetic toward such New World values.

This story also highlights the recurring tension between Holmes and Lestrade. Lestrade comes to Holmes's house to grumble about Hatty Doran's disappearance, but Holmes's response leaves him frustrated and unsatisfied. Lestrade has little time for Holmes's speculations; after all, he's been the one chasing down clues all day, while Holmes seems to have been lounging around thinking hard. "I believe in hard work and not in sitting by the fire spinning fine theories," he tells Holmes in a huff before he leaves Baker Street. Their encounter, as always, is meant to contrast Holmes—the savvy outsider—with the establishment. Still, while Holmes may be the superior intellect, he still owes a debt to Lestrade, who (accidentally) presented him with the final clue to the disappearance: the receipt from the hotel Frank Moulton was staying in.

The Adventure of the Beryl

Coronet

Summary

One snowy winter morning a large and elegantly dressed man shows up at Baker Street in a harried and agitated state. He appears to be around 50 years old. He tells Holmes and Watson his name is Alexander Holder, of the well-known London banking firm Holder & Stevenson, and he was referred to Holmes by the police. The previous day a British nobleman—Holder doesn't identify him, but claims he has "one of the highest, noblest, most exalted names in England"—visited Holder in his office to arrange a loan of £50,000, to be repaid in four days. Despite his client's standing Holder insisted he must follow official bank procedure and take some sort of collateral. The nobleman presented him with the Beryl Coronet, "one of the most precious public possessions of the empire." The coronet consists of 39 large beryls attached to a gold chasing; according to the aristocrat, its value is at least £100,000. With his collateral in hand Holder processed the loan, but after the aristocrat left Holder second-guessed his decision to make himself the guardian of such an expensive and important national treasure. Thus he decided to take the coronet home with him that evening and to keep it in his personal possession until it returned to its owner.

Holder switches to describing his household. He says he has three servants; two of them have worked with him for many years, and though the most recent hire, Lucy Parr, has only worked at the house for a few months, she has shown herself to be an honest and hard worker. Her only fault is she occasionally attracts suitors to the house because she is so pretty. Holder is a widower and has one son, Arthur, who is a "grievous disappointment." He is a wastrel and gambler and isn't good with money or work. He prefers to spend his time at an aristocratic gentleman's club, where he has fallen under the spell of an enchantingly charismatic man named Sir George Burnwell. Arthur has asked his father to loan him money to pay off his debts many times.

Holder's niece, Mary, also lives in his house. He adopted her five years ago after Holder's brother died, and their relationship is so close she refers to him as "dad." Holder is remarkably fond of Mary, whom he calls "sweet, loving, beautiful," and "my right hand." The only times she disappointed him are when she rejected (twice) marriage proposals from Arthur; Holder believes their marriage could straighten Arthur out for good.

Holder returns to his story. That evening he told Arthur and Mary he had the famous Beryl Coronet in his possession. No one else was in the room, but the door may not have been closed, and his maid Lucy may have heard his disclosure. Holder told Arthur and Mary he locked the coronet in the bureau in his dressing room, but Arthur said this isn't very secure, adding he used to open it with a different key when he was a kid. Later that night Arthur went to Holder's room and asked him for a loan of £200, saying he needed the money to repay yet another loan to someone in his club. Fed up, Holder adamantly refused. Arthur said he would be disgraced if he couldn't pay the loan back, so he would have to find the money somewhere. He sulked out of the room.

Before Holder went to sleep he checked all of the locks around the house to make sure they were secure. On his way downstairs he spotted Mary next to an open side window in the hall. When she saw Holder heading toward her she closed the window and asked if he had given Lucy permission to leave the house that night; he said he had not. Mary said Lucy was probably just talking to someone at the gate outside the house, but she had just come in through the back door. Holder was bothered by this and asserted either he or Mary should talk to Lucy the next morning. He then headed back upstairs and went to sleep.

At around two o'clock that night Holder was woken by a sound from somewhere in the house. He then heard footsteps in his dressing room. He entered the room and saw Arthur bending the coronet in some way. Arthur dropped the coronet at the sound of his father's roars. When Holder picked it up he saw that one of the gold corners and three of the beryls were missing. He accused Arthur of being a thief, but Arthur vehemently denied the charge and insisted nothing was missing. Holder called him a liar and accused him of trying to rip off another gold corner. Arthur said he could stand it no more and that he would leave the household for good the next morning. Holder, who was beside himself, said he was going to call the police on Arthur. Arthur told him to "let the police find what they can."

The screaming match woke up the household, and Mary ran into the dressing room; she fainted when she saw the coronet and then both of the men. Holder sent one of the maids out to summon the police. Arthur remained defiant after a constable and inspector arrived, and he resisted all of Holder's appeals to

confess. He was taken into custody, and his room in the house was searched, to no avail. Frantic over the missing parts of the coronet, Holder has offered a reward of £1,000. "My God, what shall I do! I have lost my honour, my gems, and my son in one night," he despairs.

Holmes sits thinking for a few minutes, and then asks Holder a number of clarifying questions. He learns Holder and Mary almost never go out, and people rarely visit the house apart from Holder's business partner and an occasional friend of Arthur's. He recalls Sir George Burnwell has visited a few times recently. Holmes says the fact that Arthur was found with the coronet doesn't necessarily mean he is the one who stole the beryls, and he adds it's possible Arthur was trying to straighten out the coronet when Holder entered the dressing room. Holder says he appreciates Holmes's attempt to exonerate Arthur, but the evidence of his guilt seems so overwhelming. Holmes wonders, however, why Arthur didn't just confess if he was guilty given he was caught red-handed. "His silence appears to me to cut both ways," Holmes asserts. Holder says the detectives have looked all over his household, including outside, but still can't find the beryls. Holmes isn't surprised to learn this; in his view it's clear the theft "strikes very much deeper than either [Holder] or the police were at first inclined to think." He argues it's very unlikely Arthur is involved in the theft given the facts.

Holmes, Watson, and Holder travel to the banker's house in Streatham, a suburb south of London. After they arrive Holmes walks painstakingly around the grounds looking for clues while Watson and Holmes wait inside. Holder's niece enters the room they're waiting in looking severely distraught. She asks Holder if he has told the police to release Arthur, but Holder says he hasn't, as "the matter must be probed to the bottom." She continues pleading with her uncle, to no avail; Holder says he is committed to finding the jewels and has even brought in a private investigator, who is currently probing around the stable lane outside the house. She raises her eyebrows at hearing this, and then greets Holmes, who has entered the house. He asks Mary a few questions. She says she didn't hear anything the previous night until her uncle started yelling, and she confirmed she fastened the windows and doors that night and they were fastened when she woke up this morning. She also confirms she saw Lucy, the maid, talking to someone the previous night, adding that this was the same maid who could have overhead Holder talk about the jewels. She says Lucy came back into the house via the kitchen door; after Mary checked to ensure the door was locked, she spotted Lucy's admirer outside, a greengrocer named Francis Prosper standing on the path some ways from the door. Holmes then asks if Prosper has a wooden leg, and Lucy's face seems to change before she confirms he does.

Holmes closely examines the windows downstairs and then heads upstairs to Holder's dressing room. He unlocks the bureau with the key—noting the lock is noiseless—and takes out the coronet. To demonstrate how incredibly strong the coronet is Holmes attempts to break off a piece of it as a shocked Holder looks on. Holmes is unable to even bend the coronet, however. He says it would be nearly impossible for someone to break off a piece of it, and if he did, it would make a sound "like a pistol shot." There's no way Arthur (or anyone) could have ripped off a piece of the coronet without waking Holder up. Holder confirms Arthur was wearing only his nightclothes when he was spotted, no shoes or slippers.

Holmes goes back outside the house to investigate. He asks the rest of the party to stay inside, lest they mess up the tracks in the snow. After an hour he comes back into the house, and tells Holder he must return to Baker Street, but the banker should visit him the next day. Holder affirms Holmes may spare no expense to get the stones back. Holmes and Watson return to Baker Street, and the detective changes into the disguise of "a common loafer." He returns a few hours later, and tells Watson he has been back to the Streatham area, but did not visit the Holder's house. He changes back into his normal clothes and then heads back out. The next morning Watson sees Holmes at breakfast. Before they can talk, Holder shows up at the house. He is crestfallen—even worse off than he was the previous day. He tells Holmes and Watson he discovered that morning that Mary has run away. She left a cryptic note for him apologizing for "[bringing] trouble upon" Holder and "this terrible misfortune." Holder wonders if this is a suicide note, but Holmes says it's not, and it's "perhaps the best possible solution." He asks Holder to write a check for £4,000. After the banker writes the check, Holmes goes to his desk and pulls out the coronet's missing gold section and three beryls. Holder is overjoyed at the sight.

Holmes asks Holder to apologize to his son, Arthur, who has actually acted nobly throughout the ordeal. He proceeds to explain his findings to the confused banker. He starts by explaining that Mary, Holder's beloved niece, has come under the spell of Sir George Burnwell, Arthur's charismatic friend from his club, and the pair has taken off. Holder is incredulous, but Holmes explains Burnwell "is one of the most dangerous

men in England." He used Mary—as he had used so many women before. When Holder came downstairs and saw Mary at the window two nights ago, she was discussing the coronet with Burnwell. She used Lucy's meet-up with the greengrocer (which really happened) as a cover story.

Later that night Arthur was awoken by Mary's footsteps outside his door. He quietly followed her into Holder's dressing room and then watched in horror as she took the coronet out of the bureau and handed it off to someone through the downstairs window. He felt he couldn't intervene at that moment because it would implicate Mary—with whom he was deeply in love—but he ran downstairs and out the door, barefoot, and chased after her co-conspirator. He caught up with Burnwell and the two men fought over the coronet; drops of Burnwell's blood dripped into the snow. As Arthur pulled the coronet off Burnwell there was a loud snap, and Arthur ran home with the jewelry. He was attempting to straighten it when Holder woke up and saw him. Despite Holder's insults, Arthur refused to explain what had happened in order to protect Mary.

At Holder's house Holmes examined the tracks in the snow in the lane outside the home. He noticed a pair of boot tracks leading toward and from the house, and a pair of footprints, going away from the house, on top of the boot tracks. The boot tracks led from the downstairs window and through the lane—to a spot with bloodstains. (He also saw the greengrocer's benign tracks.) Further inspection inside the house made the plot, and Arthur's innocence, clear to Holmes. Once he figured out whom Arthur struggled with in the snow, he would find the missing coronet piece. By process of deduction Holmes settled on Burnwell as the culprit. It's unlikely Arthur would have sacrificed himself on behalf of one of the maids, and Burnwell was known to Holmes "as being a man of evil reputation among women." Holmes traveled to Burnwell's house in his loafer disguise. He befriended Burnwell's valet, who informed him Burnwell was injured the previous night. Holmes was even able to buy Burnwell's boots off the man, which perfectly matched the tracks in the snow outside Holder's house. Holmes returned to Burnwell's house that night dressed in his normal clothes. Holmes said he would pay £1,000 for each stone, but Burnwell explained he had already sold them—for £200 each. After Holmes promised Burnwell he wouldn't report him, Burnwell gave him the address of the man who bought the stones; Holmes bought them from this man for £1,000 each. With the stones securely in his possession, he visited Arthur in prison to talk, and then returned home.

Analysis

Holmes earns his bread in this adventure, which is less of an armchair riddle than many of his other commissions. Over the course of two days he pounds the pavement doing old-fashioned investigative work. He travels twice to the Holder's house from Baker Street, twice to Sir George Burnwell's home, once to the coronet-fragment buyer, and once to the prison where Arthur is being held. His return to Baker Street, he says, comes "after what I may call a really hard day's work."

Because of the case's complexity, Holmes must utilize every effort and trick at his disposal. At the Holder home he pores painstakingly over physical evidence with his magnifying glass and imagination. He even slips into disguise in order to get intelligence on Sir George Burnwell. He is in total sleuth mode, sniffing out the details of the coronet mystery one clue at a time. Holder can't quite make sense of Holmes's questioning and running around. To him it's obvious Arthur is the culprit; after all, he was caught literally holding the broken coronet. Holmes disagrees, saying, "To me it seems exceedingly complex."

Fortunately, he gets an assist from Mother Nature. The snow is as much a character in this story as anyone else, as it reveals critical information about the theft. It exonerates Arthur Holder and the wooden-legged greengrocer, and it incriminates Sir George Burnwell. Only Holmes, however, has the sense to consider the snow for clues. Until Holmes explains his findings at the end of the story, Alexander Holder and Watson (and most readers, no doubt) remain convinced Arthur has committed the crime.

Burnwell is depicted as a perfectly dastardly villain, a sweet-talking sociopath whose moral rot is directly proportional to his charisma. Even Alexander Holder, a distinguished and wealthy professional, finds he can't resist Burnwell's charms, though he knows the fellow is bad news; Holder calls him a "brilliant talker" and a "man of great personal beauty." To an outsider such as Holmes, it's not very surprising Burnwell could (successfully) prey on someone like Mary, Holder's "sweet, loving, beautiful" niece. As a master scholar of human nature, Holmes realizes the powerful effects of romantic love. "I have no doubt that [Mary] loved you," he tells Holder, "but there are women in whom the love of a lover extinguishes all other loves."

The young rake's reputation is deserved, for he ultimately betrays the Holders in three ways: by attempting to steal the coronet; by letting Arthur take the fall for his crime; and by successfully stealing the beloved Mary away from the family.

The Adventure of the Copper Beeches

Summary

Holmes and Watson discuss previous cases. As Watson observes, Holmes's cherry-wood pipe is out during the discussion, a signal "he [is] in a disputatious rather than a meditative mood" (for the latter, he reserves his clay pipe). Holmes complains his practice "seems to be degenerating into an agency for recovering lost lead pencils and giving advice to young ladies from boarding schools." To prove his point, he passes to Watson a letter that arrived in the morning from a woman named Violet Hunter. She is seeking advice about whether or not she should accept a governess position that was offered to her, and it says she will be stopping by Baker Street that day.

As if on cue, the doorbell rings and Hunter enters. She introduces herself and explains she has come to Holmes because she doesn't have any relatives to consult with. She says she has been a governess for five years, but two months ago the family she had been working for moved to North America. In need of money and work, she recently visited a governess-placement agency in West London. At the agency she sat for an interview with the manager, Miss Stoper, and a potential client, a smiling and very fat man. When she entered the room the man "gave quite a jump in his chair" and immediately informed Stoper that Hunter was his choice. Despite her modest knowledge of French and German, the man offered her £100 per annum in exchange for taking care of a single child. The offer seemed exorbitant given the relatively modest responsibility and the fact that Hunter had received £4 per month at her previous job.

The man said he lived in a country house in Hampshire, five miles away from the town of Winchester. He explained that while the tasks were mostly straightforward—help bring up a six-year-old son and assist the man's wife—the family had a few additional requests. They would like Hunter to wear a dress they give her and to cut her hair short. The demands left Hunter flabbergasted; while she was willing to wear the dress, she was not willing to cut her hair, so she declined the offer and returned home. After seeing her bare cupboards and bills on the table, however, she decided it was silly to reject the position on account of the family's "strange fads," especially one that paid so well. Two days later she resolved to return to the agency, but before she left she received a letter from the man, Jephro Rucastle. Rucastle said his wife badly wanted Hunter to work for them, so they were raising their offer to £120 a year for humoring their fads. He said they would like her to wear an electric blue dress in the mornings, but rather than buy one she may wear an old dress of the Rucastles' daughter, who has gone to live in Philadelphia. She will, of course, also have to cut her hair.

Hunter asks Holmes what she should do. In typical understatement he says, "I confess it is not the situation which I should like to see a sister of mine apply for," but adds he has no idea what to make of the situation because he has "no data." Holmes worries the abnormally large payment is a red flag, but Hunter rationalizes accepting the job: the eccentric request is probably because of Mrs. Rucastle, who is probably mentally ill, and after all, it *is* a lot of money. Holmes assures her she may contact him any time if she's ever in danger. She thanks Holmes for his offer and goes home to write to Rucastle—and cut her hair. After she leaves Holmes tells Watson he will be surprised if they don't hear from her before long.

As Holmes predicted he receives a telegram from Hunter only two weeks later, asking him to come to the Black Swan Hotel in the town of Winchester the following day, and ending with the plea "Do come! I am at my wit's end." Watson and Holmes take the train to Winchester the following morning. It's a pleasant spring day, and Watson comments on how beautiful the countryside looks. Holmes strongly disagrees, saying that when he sees isolated houses, he sees crimes being committed with impunity, away from watchful eyes.

Holmes and Watson meet Hunter in a sitting room at the hotel, and she explains why she contacted Holmes. She says neither Mr. Rucastle nor his wife has actually mistreated her, but their bizarre conduct has been making her uneasy. As Rucastle said, the family lives in a large country house named Copper Beeches (so-named for the group of copper-colored beech

trees in front). Mrs. Rucastle isn't mentally ill; she's a "silent, pale-faced woman" who appears around 30 years old, significantly younger than her husband, who seems to be in his mid-40s. Mr. Rucastle is a widower, and his daughter is from his first marriage. According to Mr. Rucastle, his daughter—who Hunter thinks is at least 20—was uneasy around her stepmother because they are so close in age. Mrs. Rucastle was completely inoffensive, "a nonentity," but occasionally she burst out in crying fits. She is a devoted mother to her six-year-old son, a mean and spoiled-rotten brat who takes pleasure in hurting small animals. A pair of servants, a married couple named the Tollers, also live in the house. Mr. Toller is frequently drunk, and Mrs. Toller seems to be humorless and quiet.

Three days after Hunter's arrival, the Rucastles asked Hunter to try on the blue dress Mr. Rucastle had mentioned in his letter. The dress, which was laid out for Hunter in her bedroom, was a remarkably perfect fit. The couple then asked Hunter to sit in a chair next to one of the huge windows in the drawing room, a large space in the front of the house that overlooked the front lawn. The chair was turned around so Hunter faced the room. While she sat, Mr. Rucastle told different stories she found completely hilarious. This continued for an hour. This "performance" was repeated exactly two days later, except after telling funny stories for a while Mr. Rucastle directed Hunter to read a book out loud, which she did for 10 minutes.

Because her back was turned toward the window, Hunter wondered what was happening behind her, outside. During a subsequent performance, she took with her a small shard of glass, which she used to sneak glances behind her. On her second look, she saw a bearded man in a gray suit looking toward her. Mrs. Rucastle seemed to recognize that Hunter had seen something, however, and she dramatically objected to Mr. Rucastle that "there is an impertinent fellow upon the road there who stares up at Miss Hunter." Mr. Rucastle told Hunter to turn around and wave the man away; as she did so he dropped the blinds. Hunter has not been asked to stage her performance again since the incident.

Hunter offers other seemingly random tidbits about life at Copper Beeches. She learned there is an enormous and menacing mastiff that is let out to prowl the property at night. One night, while inspecting a chest of drawers in her room, she unlocked the bottom drawer and found a coil of hair that perfectly matched her own. Her most unsettling discovery, however, occurred in the wing of the house that was kept locked at all times. The door to it faces the door to the Tollers' quarters. One day, while Hunter was walking up the stairs, she came across Mr. Rucastle, who was exiting the mysterious locked door. He passed her wordlessly but appeared to be uncharacteristically agitated. When Hunter took the child outside for a walk a bit later, she walked around the house to casually inspect the wing from the outside. She noticed four windows; three were dirty, and one was shuttered. While she was walking, Mr. Rucastle came over to her and apologized for not acknowledging her on the stairs. She accepted his apologies, and then inquired about the rooms in the wing, a question that "surprised" and "startled" Rucastle; he responded that he kept a darkroom up there.

Hunter tells Holmes her interest in seeing inside the forbidden area only grew stronger—maybe because of her "woman's instinct"—and she determined to find her way in at the first opportunity. Her opportunity arrived the day before, when she sent her telegram to Holmes. The Tollers had access to the wing, and the previous day a drunken Mr. Toller left his keys in the lock; Hunter snuck in. She walked down an empty passage, and then turned right. This passage contained three rooms. The first and the third were empty, but the middle room was secured with bars and a padlock. This was the same passage she had viewed from outside during her walk, and the barricaded door aligned with the shuttered window. While Hunter was contemplating what was behind the barricade, she heard footsteps coming from within the room and seemed to make out a shadow at the bottom of the door. Terrified, she ran out of the wing —and into Mr. Rucastle.

She told Rucastle the room's quiet spooked her, not mentioning what she heard or saw. At first Rucastle comforted her, but then his tone changed and he warned that if she goes into the wing again he will "throw [her] to the mastiff." She went into town, half a mile away, and sent Holmes the telegraph asking for his help.

She tells Holmes she has to get back to the house by three o'clock, and then she will be watching the child that evening, while the Rucastles are out. Holmes asks if Mr. Toller is still drunk and if the house has a wine cellar with a lock; Hunter affirms both. Holmes comes up with a plan: he and Watson will come to Copper Beeches at seven o'clock, by which point the Rucastles should be gone and Mr. Toller will still be out of commission. He instructs Hunter to ask Mrs. Toller for something from the cellar, and then lock her in. Hunter signs on to the plan.

Holmes asserts that Hunter has clearly been used to impersonate whoever is locked in the room, who he thinks must be Rucastle's 20-something daughter. The scheme must be intended to drive away the man she saw through the drawing-room window, Holmes reasons. She was made to laugh to demonstrate how great everything is, and she was instructed to wave him off to show she had no use for him. Meanwhile, the mastiff, which guards the house at night, keeps the man away.

At seven o'clock Holmes and Watson meet Hunter at the front of the house. Mrs. Toller is locked in the cellar, and her husband is snoring on the rug. Hunter opens the door to the wing with Mr. Toller's keys, and the group makes their way to the padlocked room. When they arrive, though, none of the keys work, and no sound comes from the room. Watson and Holmes push through the door, but the room is empty; the skylight, however, is open. Holmes climbs up to the roof and sees a ladder perched against the house. He says Mr. Rucastle must have figured out Hunter's plan and pulled the prisoner out through the skylight. Hunter, however, says there was no ladder when the Rucastles left.

Footsteps are heard, and the group goes back into the room; Watson takes out his pistol. Mr. Rucastle appears at the door and then looks at the skylight. He screams at the group and then runs back down the stairs after yelling "you are in my power, I'll serve you!" As they head downstairs to close the door they hear the mastiff howl, and then a human scream. The group runs outside, followed by Mr. Toller, who had recently woken up, and Watson shoots the dog, which is attacking Mr. Rucastle. They bring Rucastle back into the house, and Watson treats him. Mrs. Toller enters the room, explaining Mr. Rucastle let her out of the cellar when he arrived. She tells Hunter she should have let her in on her plans, "for I would have told you that your pains were wasted."

She then explains what happened to the daughter, Alice, starting from the beginning. She says the girl has been unhappy since her father remarried, but the trouble really started after she met Mr. Fowler, the man whom Hunter saw outside the house. Alice had inherited money from her mother's will, but her father had always controlled it. Her marriage to Fowler, however, would take the money out of her father's hands, so Mr. Rucastle tried to get Alice to sign the will over to him. She refused, but his constant needling provoked a bout of "brain fever" in the girl (which led to the need to cut her hair). Despite all of this, Fowler remained loyal to her. To get rid of him once and for all, the Rucastles imprisoned Alice and hired Hunter to unwittingly impersonate the girl.

Holmes, who knows where this is going, finishes the story. He says the determined Mr. Fowler convinced Mrs. Toller by "certain arguments, metallic or otherwise" to help him out, and thus she ensured a ladder was in place and her husband was passed out drunk this evening, while the Rucastles were out. Alice escaped from the room by climbing up the ladder and out the skylight into Fowler's arms.

Although the details of the case have all been presented, the narrative returns to Watson's explanation of what has happened to the various parties involved. Mr. Rucastle survived his mauling, but has become an invalid and subject to the care of his wife. Mr. Fowler and Alice Rucastle were married, and Hunter now runs a private school.

Analysis

This story begins with an unusually long discussion between Holmes and Watson before the actual mystery begins. Perhaps it's because Holmes has his cherry-wood pipe out, which signals to Watson (and the reader) that the detective is in an argumentative mood. The debate centers around how Watson has presented Holmes's adventures; Holmes, who is in an atypically argumentative mood, criticizes Watson for presenting the cases in narrative form rather than as a "course of lectures." He also complains Watson has chronicled too many cases in which no crimes were technically committed at all: the Irene Adler affair, the account of the beggar with the twisted lip, and so on. He argues that in avoiding the sensational, Watson may have focused excessively on the trivial. There is a good deal of situational irony in this statement, given Holmes's famously obsessive interest in trivial details. Perhaps Holmes is just in a bad mood, especially after his letter from Hunter, whose reasons for consulting him—advice on her governess job—seem completely frivolous to him. Regardless, the long (and somewhat tense) philosophical exchange and numerous references to earlier cases are atypical.

This story punctures the myth of pure, idyllic rural life. Holmes's statements about the countryside, which he makes during the train ride to Winchester, foreshadow the sordid discovery Miss Hunter makes. Country houses, which Watson finds so charming, "always fill [Holmes] with a certain horror." As

Holmes elaborates with remarkable astuteness, "I look at them, and the only thought which comes to me is a feeling of their isolation and of the impunity with which crime may be committed there." This is exactly what has happened at Copper Beeches, the ever-so-lovely Rucastle estate: Mr. and Mrs. Rucastle have been keeping their daughter Alice locked away in a room.

In the city, Holmes argues, social pressure forces people to respond to crime, thereby reducing it. Had Hunter been working for a family in the city of Winchester, Holmes says, "I should never have had a fear for her." Holmes's argument—that the city is safer (and thus more desirable) than the country—is interesting, especially because Holmes's entire career revolves around solving crimes, mostly in the city of London. His investigations take him through slums, rough docks, opium dens, and other shabby places, but yet he feels the countryside is more perilous. Perhaps the ordeal of Alice Rucastle is the best piece of evidence to support this argument.

Several other stories in the collection echo this argument. "The Boscombe Valley Mystery," "The Five Orange Pips," "The Adventure of the Speckled Band," and "The Adventure of the Engineer's Thumb" are all set in rural areas, and they all reinforce the association between the countryside and violence. Taken together these stories indicate that Holmes (and Doyle) had a suspicious view of rural romanticism.

❛❜ Quotes

"He never spoke of the softer passions, save with a gibe and a sneer."

— Dr. John Watson, A Scandal in Bohemia

Dr. John Watson describes Sherlock Holmes, explaining that because Holmes is such a creature of reason, he looks down on emotions and feelings, seeing them as shortcomings of the unreasonable or immature.

"I have no data yet. It is a capital

mistake to theorize before one has data."

— Sherlock Holmes, A Scandal in Bohemia

Sherlock Holmes refuses to hypothesize about a crime until he has a strong base of good facts. To speculate without knowing the facts is a surefire way to fail. He repeats his belief in good "data" in many of the stories in the book.

"As a rule ... the more bizarre a thing is the less mysterious it proves to be."

— Sherlock Holmes, The Red-Headed League

In Sherlock Holmes's view sensational crimes have so many novel aspects that they easily reveal their clues. Conversely, common crimes are much more difficult to interpret.

"I have seen too much not to know that the impression of a woman may be more valuable than the conclusion of an analytical reasoner."

— Sherlock Holmes, The Man with the Twisted Lip

Sherlock Holmes says this to Mrs. St. Clair, the wife of Neville St. Clair. His argument is that "a woman's intuition" has a special power of detection. This idea is repeated in many of the stories throughout the book.

"On the contrary, Watson, you can see everything. You fail, however, to reason from what you see. You

are too timid in drawing your inferences."

— Sherlock Holmes, The Adventure of the Speckled Band

Sherlock Holmes mildly criticizes Dr. John Watson for putting too little effort into his observations. If Watson would only concentrate harder on reasoning, he would increase his observational power. He says this to his friend while they are inspecting the hat Commissionaire Peterson dropped off at Holmes's house.

"You are Holmes, the meddler."

— Dr. Grimesby Roylott, The Adventure of the Speckled Band

Dr. Grimesby Roylott spits this sentence at Sherlock Holmes while he is in Holmes's office berating the detective for speaking with his stepdaughter, Helen Stoner. The sentence is a perfect encapsulation of Holmes's life and work.

"The mystery clears gradually away as each new discovery furnishes a step which leads on to the complete truth."

— Dr. John Watson, The Adventure of the Engineer's Thumb

Watson explains how crime-solving proceeds: one clue at a time. That clue opens up another clue, and eventually the crime or the culprit is revealed.

"I believe in hard work and not in sitting by the fire spinning fine theories."

— Lestrade, The Adventure of the Noble Bachelor

Lestrade criticizes Sherlock Holmes for being an armchair detective. The Scotland Yard inspector believes crime-solving is a physical process requiring getting outside and hunting for clues. Holmes does hunt for clues, but he likes to think first about how he will go hunting.

"My God, what shall I do! I have lost my honour, my gems, and my son in one night."

— Alexander Holder, The Adventure of the Beryl Coronet

Holder expresses utter despair over the theft of the Beryl Coronet and highlights the stakes of Sherlock Holmes's crime-solving. Holder's cry is particularly dramatic, but the victims in each story undoubtedly feel the same sense of hopelessness as he does until Holmes is able to help them.

"Well, yes, of course the pay is good—too good. That is what makes me uneasy."

— Sherlock Holmes, The Adventure of the Copper Beeches

Holmes warns Miss Violet Hunter, the young governess who has asked him for advice, that the job she is considering is suspicious. His years of experience have taught him if something seems too good to be true, it most likely is.

🐦 Symbols

Pipes

Sherlock Holmes's pipes represent his cold logic. He smokes when he is stuck on a case and when he wants to philosophize. The harder the case, the more he smokes. For example, in "The Man with the Twisted Lip," Holmes stays up smoking the entire night before he is able to connect the dots between Neville St. Clair and the beggar Hugh Boone. Over the course of the evening he winds up smoking a full ounce of coarsely cut tobacco known as shag. In "The Red-Headed League" Holmes tells Watson the mystery is "a three pipe problem."

Holmes even smokes different pipes depending on his disposition. He takes out his cherry-wood pipe when he's in a "disputatious" mood, Watson informs the reader. When he's stuck in a problem, however, Holmes smokes his clay pipe. Whatever the pipe, when one is out the reader knows Holmes's mind is churning.

Violins

Violins represent Sherlock Holmes's romantic side. The detective is a master logician who is guided by reason above all else. He is suspect of love and emotions, viewing them as weaknesses that lead to bad decisions and, too often, crime. As a natural result he is almost always dispassionate, collected, and unemotional. His state, however, doesn't come entirely naturally to him—in fact he has to work to repress his emotions, Watson explains, for Holmes actually has a sensitive side he keeps buried.

This side comes out with the violin. On rare occasions Holmes will allow himself the pleasure of playing or listening to violin music. While he does he seems to transform into an entirely different person—someone with passion. His head nods along with the music, and he becomes overtaken by the pleasure of the moment—the very vice he rails against when he is in detective mode.

🎭 Themes

Mystery

The Adventures of Sherlock Holmes shows that the world

works in mysterious ways—or rather, appears to. Over the course of *The Adventures of Sherlock Holmes*, the detective finds himself entangled in one bizarre plot after the next. Holmes confronts a scam organization claiming to honor red-headed men; a stepfather who disguises himself as a suitor to his stepdaughter; a thief who hides a precious jewel in a goose; and a family who hires someone to impersonate their daughter—whom they keep locked in a room—among other schemes.

While life is indeed strange, it is not actually incomprehensible, at least not for the determined and capable sleuth. At face value, all of the above plots appear to be completely random, cruel schemes in a scary world that makes no sense. To Holmes, however, they can be explained: by greed, jealously, anger, and other social causes.

Sherlock Holmes is able to solve the mysteries that so confound his clients, but he is one detective against the world. Most people don't have access to Holmes or other competent mystery-solvers, so their unresolved problems feel incomprehensible. When Holmes solves a mystery, he is providing a cosmic resolution, because he is able to reassure his clients—and, importantly, his readers—that, in fact, things happen for a reason. The world is mysterious and absurd—only to the untrained eye. For those with the powers of observation and reasoning, it is knowable.

Justice

Sherlock Holmes is not merely a crime solver: he is a reliever of existential angst. Holmes's clients come to him because they believe they have been wronged. In many cases the official authorities have been unable to help them or give them the resolution they are seeking. They are desperate for his assistance, not only because they want to know what has happened to them, but because their beliefs in a just, coherent world are at stake. He is their last hope, a firewall between optimism and hopelessness.

The fact that Holmes solves nearly all of his cases is important, because it provides reassurance to his readers that the world is in fact just. While the plot lines in *The Adventures of Sherlock Holmes* shrewdly play on anxieties and fears of the age—in particular, the big, scary city—Holmes demonstrates they can

be overcome. Had the detective rarely solved any of his cases, it's unlikely he would be nearly as popular, because he would reinforce the fear of an unjust world, a prospect that, for many people, is too terrifying to consider. Holmes's enduring appeal is that in his hands wrongs can indeed be righted.

Camaraderie

Sherlock Holmes's relationship with Dr. John Watson demonstrates the power of friendship in a changing world. Though Watson has inferior crime-solving skills, Holmes always insists the doctor accompany him on his crime-solving missions. Watson helps Holmes work through his thinking, challenges him on different points, and provides an emotional resource to the solitary and stiff-upper-lipped sleuth. By being available for his friend, Watson is an essential part of Holmes's crime-solving toolkit.

As well the men's shared history makes Dr. Watson an invaluable asset to the detective. Holmes's cases bring him into contact with humans at their worst; he encounters liars, thieves, schemers, murderers, usurers, vengeful ex-lovers, and other damaged people who cannot be trusted. Holmes, however, knows he can always rely on his old friend. In this way readers can relate to their relationship. In an unmoored, uncertain, and seemingly unsafe world, a deep friendship is a rock of stability.

Reasoning

Sherlock Holmes is a master of deductive reasoning. In nearly every case that comes his way he seems to spend almost as much time asking questions and contemplating motives as he does physically chasing down clues. His chief weapon is his mind, which he has trained to be a cold, effective instrument that runs on logic alone. (This explains his disdain for emotional responses like passion and love, which he believes are the enemies of reason.) Through his years of studying crime and human behavior, he knows exactly what questions and information to pursue in order to solve a mystery. The message of the entire collection of stories in *The Adventures of Sherlock*

Holmes is that a powerful enough dose of reason can resolve almost any problem.

Holmes's reasoning is so effective because he has such solid data—facts and clues. "You know my method," Holmes tells Watson after the sleuth literally combs for clues in Chapter 4. "It is founded upon the observation of trifles." Throughout the story collection Holmes is constantly observing details, even seemingly insignificant ones. In his view these clues are rarely minor and so often hold the key to solving a case.

🗒 Motifs

Deception

The world of Sherlock Holmes is a world of lies. This state of affairs is necessary in any book of mysteries, but it also reveals anxieties about life during Victorian times. As people moved into cities, they were suddenly surrounded by strangers. Holmes, however, could provide something critical: the truth. Holmes's clients have been cheated and abused, misled and deceived, and he is hired to see through these deceptions to establish the truth. The deceptions Holmes's clients are subject to give each adventure its narrative thrust. Each case is a race to discover the meaning of a lie or reveal what someone is hiding, and each story reaches its climax when the deception is revealed.

Arthur Conan Doyle employs some situational irony by causing Holmes, in his crusade to establish the truth, to employ his own deceptive tricks, such as going in disguise. He dresses as a stable groom, a "loafer," and other characters in order to earn the trust of people—and then exploits it to gain information. This makes him an effective sleuth who uses deception for his own advantage.

Travel

The wealth and growth that occurred during Victorian England bequeathed to the nation a far-reaching network of rails and carriage routes. Within cities residents could hail "cabs"—carriage taxis—just like people do today. This created a mobility unknown to earlier generations, a mobility widely reflected in *The Adventures of Sherlock Holmes*. Holmes and different characters constantly travel around the city of London and often travel to distant areas of the country. Several of the characters in the stories, such as Neville St. Clair and Alexander Holder, actually commute into London each day for work by train. Still others, such as Dr. Roylott Grimesby, who lived in India, have traveled overseas.

These new opportunities, however, make Holmes's sleuthing more time-consuming, as he must leave his home base in central London to gather clues and investigate. He must also be well-informed about the wider world, since many of the cases he works on involve incidents that took place in other countries. In this respect the mobile, worldly detective is a perfect embodiment of a Victorian sleuth.

📖 Suggested Reading

Dundas, Zach. *The Great Detective: The Amazing Rise and Immortal Life of Sherlock Holmes.* New York: Houghton, 2015. Print.

McInerny, D. Q. "Sherlock Holmes: Artist of Reason." *The Philosophy of Sherlock Holmes.* Ed. Phillip Tallon and David Baggett. Louisville: U of Kentucky, 2012. N109-20. Print.

Metress, Christopher. "Holmes & Social Order." *English Literature in Transition* 41.1 (1998): 87-90. Print.

Riggs, Ransom, and Eugene Smith. *The Sherlock Holmes Handbook.* Philadelphia: Quirk, 2009. Print.

Rothman, Steven, ed. *The Standard Doyle Company: Christopher Morley on Sherlock Holmes.* New York: Fordham UP, 1993. Print.

Printed in Great Britain
by Amazon